The
MODERN RULES
of
Business Etiquette

SECOND EDITION

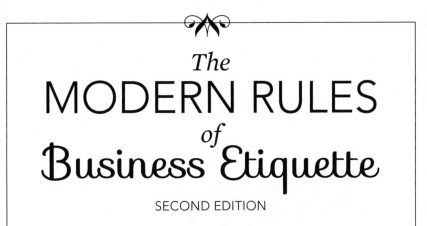

The
MODERN RULES
of
Business Etiquette

SECOND EDITION

Donna Gerson *and* David Gerson

AMERICAN BAR ASSOCIATION
**Defending Liberty
Pursuing Justice**

Cover design by Jill Tedhams/ABA Publishing.

Printed in the United States of America.

18 17 16 15 14   5 4 3 2 1

Library of Congress Cataloging-in-Publication Data

Gerson, Donna, author.
  The modern rules of business etiquette / Donna Gerson, David Gerson. -- Second edition.
     pages cm
  Includes bibliographical references.
  ISBN 978-1-62722-397-3
  1. Commercial law--Handbooks, manuals, etc. 2. Business etiquette--Handbooks, manuals, etc. 3. Etiquette--United States. I. Gerson, David, 1963- author. II. Title.
  KF319.G47 2014
  395.5'2--dc23

                                                                              2013051210

Discounts are available for books ordered in bulk. Special consideration is given to state bars, CLE programs, and other bar-related organizations. Inquire at Book Publishing, ABA Publishing, American Bar Association, 321 N. Clark Street, Chicago, Illinois 60654-7598.

www.ShopABA.org

Eunice Burns (played by Madeline Kahn):
"Don't you know the meaning
of the word 'propriety'?"

Judy Maxwell (played by Barbra Streisand):
"Propriety . . . Noun: Conformity to established
standards of behavior, or manner, suitability,
ripeness or justice. See 'etiquette.'"

From *What's Up, Doc?* (1972)

Contents

About the Authors

Donna Gerson is a former contributing editor for *Student Lawyer* magazine. She is the author of several books on professional development issues, including *Choosing Small, Choosing Smart* and *Building Career Connections*. Donna graduated from the University of Pennsylvania, earned her law degree from Temple University Beasley School of Law, and also has a master's degree in library and information sciences from the University of Pittsburgh. She served as the director of the career services office at the University of Pittsburgh School of Law between 1993 and 2001.

David Gerson is a partner in the Philadelphia office of Morgan, Lewis & Bockius LLP, where he practices in the firm's Business & Finance Practice Group. His practice focuses on representing financial and strategic buyers and sellers in mergers and acquisitions, as well as governance and general corporate matters. David earned his under-graduate degree from the University of Pennsylvania and his law degree from Harvard Law School.

Preface

Could a book about etiquette for lawyers be a bit like a book about vegetarianism for a tribe of cannibals? We think not and disagree (politely) with anyone who assumes otherwise. While there are certainly a number of excellent books on manners for the general public, there are no comprehensive resources that discuss etiquette and the legal profession specifically.

The Modern Rules of Business Etiquette will teach you the not-so-secret secrets of how to behave like a proper gentleman or lady who is also an officer of the court. Why should the rules of etiquette concern lawyers? Good manners are, simply put, good for business. No matter how brilliant your legal brain may be, if you fail to treat others with respect and kindness, then you will not enjoy the professional success you desire. Don't believe the hype: Nice lawyers—and talented professionals—finish first.

In *The Modern Rules of Business Etiquette,* you will learn the rules of good manners and the pitfalls of bad behavior, from the time you interview, through your early years as a lawyer, to partnership, and beyond. Our twelve easy-to-read chapters provide practical guidance and tips for everyone, from entry-level associates to the most senior partner. After all, it's never too late to learn good manners.

What qualifies us to write this book? A reasonable question, no doubt. David is a partner in the business and finance practice at a major international law firm, and he spends his days (and many nights and vacations) in continual telephone, email, and face-to-face contact with clients, other lawyers, staff members, outside consultants, transaction counterparts, and opposing counsel. He has served on his firm's advisory board and as the leader of his office's business and finance practice group. He sees the theory and practice of formal and informal systems of etiquette and conduct—and their positive and negative impacts—every day. Donna is a former contributing editor for *Student Lawyer* magazine and writes extensively about professional development issues. She lectures at law schools across the U.S. When visiting law schools, Donna meets with law students and recent graduates to learn first-hand about the issues and concerns weighing on the minds of those seeking jobs in a very challenging legal market. Both Donna and David have witnessed first-hand some truly appalling manners throughout the profession and have lived to tell the tale.

We've been married for over twenty-five years and have been exceedingly polite to one another, with some notable exceptions that don't bear repeating here (no matter how funny they are in hindsight). While good manners are not the sole key to our success, we believe they do count as a big plus in our lives. (Just ask our son, whose lot in life is to be reminded of the rules of etiquette constantly by us both, to his evident joy.)

We do hope you enjoy this book and gain a better understanding of the importance of good manners. We welcome your comments, so long as they are considerate in tone and well written. Donna is a sparkling presenter and witty raconteur, and she would be pleased to speak at your law firm, bar association, or law school. (David's billable hourly rate is . . . oh, never mind.) Thank you for your consideration and happy reading.

Donna and David Gerson
Philadelphia, Pa.

Chapter One

Interview Etiquette: Setting the Stage for Success

Where better to begin to apply the rules of professional etiquette than at the beginning? Your job interview sets the tone for future employment. While your academic credentials and work experience are factors taken into consideration by an employer, your behavior throughout the interview process will spell success or failure as a job candidate.

Stories abound regarding interview transgressions that smack of poor behavior, thoughtlessness, and lack of common sense (which, apparently, is less common than previously thought). A candidate with stellar credentials who is nonetheless a boor will bear the consequences of his poor behavior. Conversely, the competent academic candidate with excellent interpersonal skills and evidence of a strong work ethic may be able to sway a hiring partner's decision-making process in his favor.

The following tips will help you navigate the interview process and capitalize on your credentials:

Résumé

Your résumé provides an employer with relevant information about your academic successes, work experience, and other achievements of interest. Typically one page in length—or, for those with extensive professional backgrounds, one page for every ten years of work experience—your résumé should be printed on plain white or beige paper. Avoid brightly colored paper, fanciful designs, or anything that will bring attention to your résumé in a negative way. A two-page résumé can be acceptable so long as the most relevant information appears on the first page.

Be sure that your résumé is free from misspellings, typographical errors, and any puffery. Your goal is to present your information in an accurate and straightforward manner. Keep your font choice simple and consistent throughout. Times New Roman font is easy to read, as are Garamond and Arial. Font size should be at least 11-point, ideally 12-point; anything smaller will be difficult to read. In addition, as more employers move to scanning technology to read résumés digitally, a consistent font and font size will simplify your application process and help ensure that your data is scanned accurately.

One of the best pieces of advice for job seekers is to either visit your law school career services office or consult with someone you trust to review your résumé. It's easy to lose sight of the big picture when trying to convey personal information about yourself. The beauty of an objective outsider reading about your credentials is that you can get unvarnished feedback about whether you're saying too much or too little, or lacking in clarity. While it's tempting to make your job search a very personal journey, it does help to widen your circle and request objective feedback.

If you are emailing a résumé to an employer, consider sending the document not only as an attachment but also in the body of your email message. Despite the formatting irregularities that may result, you guarantee that a potential employer will be able to review your credentials quickly rather than waste time trying to open an attachment or risk losing the communication in the firm's spam filter. Explain yourself with a simple note saying, "For your convenience I have attached a copy of my résumé for your review and have also pasted it into the body of this message in case you have difficulty opening the attachment. Please forgive any formatting irregularities as the result of emailing this document to you."

Cover Letter

A well-written, personalized cover letter should convey your reasons for seeking employment and highlight particular skills or experiences that may be relevant to an employer. As with your résumé, avoid typographical errors, grammatical errors, and misspellings by proofreading carefully and having others review your work prior to sending. Countless applications have been tossed unceremoniously because either the firm name or the hiring partner's name has been misspelled. Don't be that person.

While space considerations prevent us from writing a long tome about cover letters, the following tips will help make your correspondence stand out in a positive way:

Try to limit your cover letter to one page, if possible. Certainly, some circumstances call for two or more pages (this may be the case for lawyers with decades of experience), but use your good judgment when it comes to longer cover letters. Remember that your cover letter is often viewed as your first writing sample; you need to construct a letter that is both succinct and compelling.

Your cover letter ought to consist of three or four well-written paragraphs that succinctly introduce you to an employer and describe your relevant credentials without reciting your résumé in its entirety.

A well-written cover letter requires a level of thoughtfulness that anticipates what a particular employer may be interested in learning about you beyond the confines of your résumé. While we live in an age of over-sharing, it surprises us how little law students are willing to share with potential employers, relying instead on academic credentials to convince an employer of one's suitability for a job. A better approach is to view your résumé and cover letter as two distinctly different, but complementary, documents that support your candidacy. Your résumé lays out your relevant experiences and achievements; your cover letter answers the question, "Why should I hire you from among all of the qualified candidates?" The answer to that very sensible question lies in connecting the dots for a potential employer through your cover letter. For example, rather than write platitudes such as "I am a very hard worker," illustrate this point with information not readily available from your résumé.

Writing Sample

Many employers request writing samples, particularly from law students and recent graduates. A writing sample offers an employer a sense of your writing style and enables you to demonstrate your facility in thinking and writing about a specific legal topic. Generally speaking, writing samples ought to be between five and ten pages in length. If you have a longer writing sample (for instance, a longer brief with three separate issues under consideration), then consider choosing one issue for presentation to an employer. A short paragraph at the beginning of the writing sample can explain that this represents one of several issues before the court.

Of course, your writing sample must be wholly your own work and not the result of a collaborative project or excessive editing by a faculty member or colleague. It's always considerate to ask permission from an employer prior to using work produced for a client as a writing sample. This is the case with private practitioners, judges, and government agencies. Ask permission first and avoid any problems later. In addition, if you are using a brief or memo that was created for an employer, be sure to redact identifying information in order to protect confidentiality and the attorney-client privilege.

Finally, know the content of your writing sample backward and forward. If you cannot discuss intelligently the issues presented in your own work, then you cannot expect an employer to have confidence in your ability to do the job.

References

Many employers ask for two or three references, either prior to the commencement of or during the interview process. Choose individuals who know your work product and your work ethic. Always ask a reference for permission to be listed as a reference *before* your interview. This way, no one is taken aback or surprised by a phone call or email requesting information about you.

Social Media Savvy

In the age of LinkedIn, Facebook, Twitter, Instagram, and YouTube, employers have been known to Google candidates and discover information unintended for a larger audience; to wit, photos from your bachelorette party, a blog that you wrote during law school, or candid observations posted online by your ex. Employers have a vested interest in making sure that new hires have reputable personas online, since your social media savvy reflects your good judgment, professionalism, and maturity. Not only hiring attorneys, but also opposing counsel, potential clients, and professional recruiters Google prospective hires. As an officer of the court, you do not want others questioning your professionalism based on some long forgotten photos that were taken at your college frat party.

Therefore, before you embark on the interview process, Google yourself to see what comes up. You should also set up a Google Alert on your name, as well as relevant topics of interest, to stay current. If you find unsavory information about yourself, then you may need to engage the services of a company such as ReputationDefender (www .reputation.com) to de-optimize certain entries and create other entries for employers to find. Of course, it's easier to think about this issue now and avoid these troubles by being extraordinarily discrete online. A little mystery can be good generally, and particularly helpful in the job search, where over-sharing can become a deal-breaker.

Your email address should similarly reflect a professional demeanor. Hence, no email addresses such as sxylwyr@gmail.com, beerpongchampion@aol.com, or janesmommy@yahoo.com. Keep it simple, professional, and neutral: your first initial and last name or first and last name. Again, a little mystery and discretion can go a long way in this world.

Social media enables job seekers to create a personal brand and build connections. If you maintain a personal web page or blog, make sure that it exudes professionalism and good taste. Nothing can be hidden on the web, and employers—as well as clients—will question your good manners (and good judgment) if they find tasteless, thoughtless, or inflammatory information posted by you or about you. A personal website or blog can be a great place to post longer or shorter versions of your résumé and personal statements. A blog or website can also help demonstrate your passion for a particular area of law.

Twitter enables you to follow postings related to the legal profession and re-tweet relevant information to your followers. Donna (@DonnaGerson) follows @AmLawDaily, @Heather_Jarvis (student debt expert), @Beyond_The_Bar, and @atlblog, to name a few law-related Twitter feeds. While she isn't going to receive "The Most Twitter Followers" merit badge anytime soon, Donna finds that Twitter allows her to scan for newsworthy items daily and pass along relevant news to her network.

LinkedIn is fast becoming an essential online marketing tool for legal employers, lawyers, and law students. LinkedIn enables you to build an online professional network and share ideas. Treat LinkedIn and other social media as an opportunity to showcase your professionalism and discretion. Employ common sense to your use of social media and remember that what happens online can have lasting consequences.

Scheduling the Interview

When an employer or staff member calls to schedule an interview, you are "on stage" going forward. Accordingly, your manners—good, bad, or nonexistent—will be scrutinized from now on. From the moment the email arrives or the telephone rings to arrange a time to meet, you must exercise proper etiquette. Proper etiquette means:

A Prompt Response

When you are interviewing, consider yourself "in play" 24/7. This means regular checking of your voicemail (home and mobile phones), email, and regular mail. Long lapses responding to employers will be considered a sign of indifference and translates into bad manners. The day you receive an invitation to interview, respond immediately.

An Enthusiastic Response

When you respond, do so with enthusiasm. Nothing creates a bad impression faster than the candidate who calls to schedule an interview with a poor attitude. While you should never fake your demeanor, you should summon a level of enthusiasm about the prospect of receiving an interview and convey that to a potential employer. "Thank you for inviting me to interview with your firm. I would be delighted to schedule a time to visit your offices" goes a lot farther than "Oh, I guess I have to schedule a time to come in now."

Plan Ahead

When scheduling an interview, be sure to ask for directions (if it's not a location with which you are familiar) and reiterate the date and time of the meeting to the person with whom you are speaking. Some employers—judges, for instance—might ask job candidates to research and draft a short brief as part of the interview process. Ask what will be required and plan ahead. Also, ask if the employer needs any additional information at the time of the interview, such as a writing sample, transcript, list of references, or other documentation. Remember: Proper preparation prevents poor performance.

Reimbursement for Travel

If an employer offers to reimburse you for travel to an initial or second interview, review the parameters for reimbursement. What is covered? Does the law firm handle the travel and hotel arrangements or does the interviewee?

To whom should receipts be sent? Is there a form that must be used? What is the timeline for reimbursement? What are reasonable costs for the purposes of reimbursement? Understanding these details helps avoid any misunderstandings that can be construed as poor etiquette. Countless stories are told of interviewees who displayed poor etiquette—and did not receive a job offer as a result—with reimbursement requests for first-class travel, nightclub visits, adult movies on pay-per-view, or raids on the minibar at the hotel.

Conduct Research

Before arriving for your interview, research the employer to understand its key practice areas, significant cases, representative clients, and recent news about the firm. This information can be obtained from a firm's website, or by using Westlaw or LexisNexis®. By understanding key information about your potential employer, you can formulate intelligent questions, convey information that may be relevant to the employer, and form a positive first impression.

If you are given the names of the lawyers with whom you will be interviewing, also take the time to research basic information about each of them: college, law school, practice area, key cases or deals, any publications, and noteworthy awards. While the roster of lawyers with whom you will be meeting may change on short notice, at the very least you can be familiar with many of the people you may meet and can plan ahead.

Arrive on Time

If you have planned ahead, then you should arrive on time (translation: about ten minutes before the interview start time, but no earlier than that). Tardiness will be viewed negatively and conveys both poor etiquette and poor planning on your part.

Appropriate Dress

In most cases, interview apparel will consist of the traditional dark-colored suit, white shirt, conservative shoes, and minimal jewelry. Tattoos and body piercings (other than earrings for women) ought to be covered discretely from public view. When faced with the dilemma of business casual, opt for more formal rather than less formal attire. Too casual can be misconstrued as non-serious. Carry a briefcase or portfolio containing extra copies of your résumé, writing sample, transcript, and list of references.

A Firm Handshake

The appropriate mode of greeting during an interview (or any business situation, for that matter) is a firm handshake. It may sound silly, but practice shaking hands to make sure your handshake is firm, but not bone-crushing, and that your hand is dry, not clammy. You may not wave hello to people in interviews, nod your head in their general direction, or bow at the waist. Extend your right hand with confidence and shake the other person's hand in greeting while saying, "It's a pleasure to meet you." Look the person in the eye and smile. Eye contact and a genuine smile help to establish rapport and demonstrate confidence.

Staff Relations

Treat everyone you meet during the course of your interview with the utmost respect and kindness. From the managing partner to the filing room clerk, every single person deserves to be treated with respect. The sign of a true lady or gentleman lies in his or her ability to treat every single person with the same level of deference, regardless of position. Everyone deserves direct eye contact, a smile, and a handshake. Everyone you meet during the interview process will someday have to interact with you during a routine business day. Therefore, your interview day should be your opportunity to lay the groundwork for a mutually respectful work environment.

Ask Appropriate Questions

During the course of your interview, you will be asked by an employer, "Do you have any questions for me?" Unless you do not want to receive an offer, come prepared with questions to ask. "No, I don't have any questions," is not a proper response. Lack of curiosity indicates lack of interest, and it's your job to appear interested and enthusiastic.

If you have engaged in research prior to your interview, then you ought to have several thoughtful questions to ask. Avoid asking questions that would involve a simple yes or no answer; instead, focus on asking questions pertaining to a person's motivation or reasoning. The following questions invite an employer to speak about substantive issues:

- "What led you to decide to practice labor law?"
- "Do you find that your mentor program helps retain promising lawyers?"
- "Tell me what you enjoy most about your work at this firm."

Inappropriate questions are those that may embarrass, surprise, or call into question your work ethic. The essence of good etiquette is to put people at ease. Hence, avoid questions relating to marital status, race, religion, salary, vacation time, or parental leave. Issues relating to remuneration, billable hours, and benefits will be discussed in detail after the offer is made. In many cases, particularly with large firms, this information is publicly available from the *National Association for Legal Career Professionals (NALCP) Directory of Legal Employers.*

Ideally, the best interviews are conversations in which you can learn about the firm, and the lawyer with whom you are meeting, and form an opinion about whether this place would be a good fit for you (as well as vice versa). A colleague once described a good interview using the image of a beach ball being tossed gently from one person to another. You neither want to hog the conversation nor sit frozen in your chair awaiting the next interrogatory; don't hold the ball, and don't let it hit you in the head. Allow the conversation to flow by being interested and interesting to be around.

Telephone or Skype Interviews

Some employers offer telephone or Skype interviews to screen candidates. While Skype or telephone interviews save travel costs and can be conducted on short notice, they offer challenges to the interviewee not only from a practical, but also from an etiquette, perspective. Interviewing in person is optimal, but if your only option is to conduct an interview via Skype or telephone, the following suggestions will help create the best impression under the circumstances:

- Prepare carefully. As with any interview, you should prepare carefully and conduct the necessary research beforehand. If you are not familiar with Skype, then rehearse with a practice interview and test the technology so that you are comfortable.

- Lights, camera, action. Whether you interview via Skype or telephone, it helps to pretend that you are meeting in person. Dress in interview attire and make sure the room where you are conducting your interview remains quiet and undisturbed. Place a sign on the door that says, "Interview in progress"; if you are a student, ask if your career services office has a quiet space that you can borrow. For Skype interviews, make sure the background behind you is not a distraction.

Whether you are on camera or on the telephone, pay attention to your posture and be sure to smile, since this will give you confidence. For Skype interviews, remember to make eye contact with the camera.

- Speak clearly and slowly. If you tend to speak quickly, you should pay attention to the pace of your delivery and slow things down. Breathe between sentences.

- Listen attentively. Focus on the questions you are asked and demonstrate active listening skills by nodding your head in agreement (when appropriate) and interjecting "yes," "certainly," or "I understand" at intervals to let the interviewer know that you are there and actively engaged in the conversation. To focus yourself during the interview, turn off any browsers, ringers, instant-messaging chats, or other distractions.

- Close with confidence. Since there is no handshake at the conclusion of a telephone or Skype interview, you need to plan a strong conclusion that you can rehearse in advance. Be sure to thank the interviewer for his or her time, reiterate your interest in the firm, and state that you look forward to a subsequent conversation in person.

Meals

During the interview process, members of the firm often take candidates out to lunch or dinner. The meal can be a chance to demonstrate one's excellent etiquette skills or (far worse) showcase one's utter lack of good manners. To avoid the latter, here are some tips to guide you:

- If you have dietary restrictions or food allergies, do let the employer know in advance. Advance warning will enable the employer to choose a restaurant best suited to your needs.
- Drink in moderation, if at all. One serving of alcohol at dinner will suffice. More than one drink and you may lose your focus. These days, imbibing alcohol at lunch is *verboten*. Follow the lead of the most senior person regarding alcohol consumption, but always err on the side of the teetotaler. Of course, if you do not consume alcohol at all, then simply demur and sip water or a soft drink instead.
- Choose foods that are easy to eat. Avoid saucy or oily dishes, spaghetti, or anything that will splatter or drip. This is probably not the time to order the fajitas or the shrimp scampi.
- Engage in conversation. Your role in the interview meal is not to indulge in a fine meal (save that for

another time), but to engage in delightful, relaxed conversation with potential colleagues. Stay alert and in interview mode throughout the meal.

- Do not order the most expensive dish on the menu. The interview meal is not the time to order the caviar or the chef's tasting menu (unless you're following the lead of your hosts).

- The interview meal is a bad time to experiment with unfamiliar foods. If you've never indulged in a raw bar before, then it's probably wise to skip the oysters on the half shell. A colleague of ours tried oysters for the first time during her interview lunch, and later the oysters ended up being projectile vomited during the afternoon interview session. While she did receive an offer (and a complimentary overnight hotel stay with dry cleaning services, to boot), it's not a recommended course of action.

- Be friendly, but not familiar. Despite the lovely atmosphere and the tasty meal, you are still interviewing—remain focused and do not lapse into too familiar territory. Often firms will send associates who are close to you in age. You may feel relaxed and comfortable discussing things more openly with them than with a more senior lawyer. Avoid becoming too familiar with your meal partners, however; this is still an interview.

- A popular hostess once said, "The key to good conversation is to be interesting and interested." You can make yourself interesting by contributing to the conversation. Think about sharing your insights about your favorite books and movies, special travel plans in the future, or interesting hobbies. In addition, focus on being interested in what others say at the dining table. Listen attentively, lean in, and don't "one-up" or interrupt.

- Use your table manners, always. Napkin on lap when you are seated. Water glass to your right. Bread plate to your left. If you need a refresher course in dining etiquette or feel nervous, get tutored beforehand. Many career services offices are now offering dining etiquette programs (complete with a meal), so if you are a student and you see a program on campus, consider attending.

- Treat the servers with the utmost respect. How you treat others reflects on you. As two veterans of the hospitality industry (David was a busboy and a cook, and Donna had several stints at Philadelphia dining establishments in her wild youth), we know that the people serving and cooking are smart and hardworking and deserve your respect.

- Doggie bags are a no-no at interview meals. When dining with friends and family, feel free to take home the leftovers. We insist. When dining with a prospective employer, the food stays in the restaurant, as do the salt and pepper shakers.

Cocktails

Occasionally, when time is limited, you may be treated to a drink at a local bar, either in lieu of or in addition to an interview meal. Proceed with caution. One drink, if you consume alcohol, is probably the most you should enjoy while interviewing. After one alcoholic beverage, switch to water or a soft drink; a club soda with a lemon or lime wedge masquerades marvelously as a cocktail. Loose lips may sink ships, but too much alcohol will torpedo your interview forever.

Say Thank You

"Thank you." These are perhaps the most important two words in the English language. Express your thanks both verbally and in writing. When you are leaving the restaurant or the office at the conclusion of your interview, shake hands with the interviewers and say, "Thank you, I'm so pleased we met so that I could learn more about your firm." Within twenty-four hours, send a typed thank you letter to the person who organized your interview (at large firms this person would be the legal personnel director). Depending on the circumstances, a handwritten note may also be acceptable. Email communications can be acceptable, too. Use your good judgment when drafting written or email communications, but in any event, convey your sincere thanks promptly and in properly spelled and grammatically correct writing.

Accepting an Offer

After successfully navigating the interview process, the next potential etiquette pitfall comes at the time you accept an offer. When you receive an offer, typically the hiring partner or human resources director will explain the terms of employment: your start date, your salary, benefits, and the like. The employer will also give you a deadline to accept the offer. While there is room to negotiate particular issues (although in the case of a recent law school graduate, this is unlikely to be the case for material terms of employment), you should honor the acceptance deadline. Ignoring the deadline or simply ignoring the offer are both signs of poor manners and poor judgment.

If you are a law student faced with multiple offers of employment, follow the Principles and Standards for Law Placement and Recruitment Activities set forth by NALP (www.nalp.org) regarding the number of offers that can be held at one time. When rejecting an offer, do so with care and sincerity. The law firm you reject today may be the employer of your dreams tomorrow.

When you do accept an offer, do so in a timely manner and with enthusiasm. Nothing starts an employment relationship off on the wrong foot faster than mishandling the acceptance process.

Declining an Offer

When you must decline an offer, do so by telephone if at all possible, followed by an appropriate, written correspondence. Do not telephone the employer after regular business hours and leave a message on voicemail. Have the decency to call during business hours and speak directly with the appropriate person to deliver your message, however disappointing it may be to the employer.

An email note declining an offer has the feel of informality, and is frowned upon by most recruiting professionals. Moreover, no matter how accurate your email program's spell-check function may seem to be, the chances of an error in an email are simply too great; while we all hopefully will have many choices of potential work environments, and thus the chance to choose not to work at one or more of them, there is no need to burn a bridge through a careless email containing typographical or grammatical errors that causes the rejected employer to say, "Good thing we didn't wind up taking that one; we dodged a bullet."

Rescinding an Acceptance

Avoid the drama of "cold feet" after accepting an offer of employment. This type of poor behavior will set a negative tone whether you ultimately accept the offer or rescind your acceptance. Whether you are seeking a job immediately following graduation or switching firms mid-career, you ought to have considered all of the pros and the cons prior to accepting an offer of employment.

Certainly, there are circumstances that require a change of plans. For example, a spouse or partner relocating to another coast, illness, or other catastrophic life change can dictate a change in employment plans. The decision to rescind an acceptance should be approached with the greatest care, since retracting an acceptance reflects poorly on you as an individual and will not be forgotten.

Chapter Two

Office Etiquette: Working With Those More Senior

Law is a service business, within which our highest priority is to serve our clients. That priority extends from the most senior lawyer in each attorney-client relationship through the people in the mailroom, and embraces everyone in-between. Every successful lawyer recognizes that, while technical brilliance can carry you far down the field, service excellence enables you to cross the goal line.

The junior lawyer, especially when working in a larger, institutional setting, may be tempted at first to see clients as remote, otherworldly beings. In fact, though, clients are all around them: Clients are behind the memos they write, the depositions they attend, the due diligence documents they review; clients are the recipients of the timesheet entries they compose; ultimately, clients are writing the paychecks they cash (and then promptly use to pay their law school debt). More immediately, junior lawyers have a separate, often insistent set of clients readily at hand: As a junior lawyer, the more senior lawyers with whom you work are your clients.

As with external clients, your primary goal in working with those more senior than you should be to make the job of the more senior attorney easier, by being eager, appropriate, honest, timely, available, and responsive; the etiquette of working with more senior lawyers revolves around each of those specific behaviors. If you can master not just the substance, but also the style, of serving in a more junior role, then you'll truly squeeze the most out of each experience, quickly assume the higher levels of responsibility you seek, and at the same time gain valuable insights into how to manage client relationships and entire matters, and how to supervise more junior attorneys yourself someday.

Let's look at some specific situations in which junior lawyers often find themselves, and try to discern some of the "do's and don'ts" of working in a more junior role:

"The Importance of Being Earnest"

Imagine that you're a junior attorney, recently embarked upon your career, sitting at your desk and waiting for the phone to ring (perhaps dreading that it will). When the call does come, don't answer with trepidation or resignation;

put a smile on your face and a song in your heart, and say, "I'm happy to help in any way; I'll be right down." Come prepared; bring a pad and a pen at all times. When you meet with the more senior attorney, take a seat and sit up in your chair; do not slouch. Look the assigning attorney in the eye. Pay rapt attention, look eager, and take good notes as the assignment is given.

Wait until the assignment has been laid out, then ask any questions that have occurred to you during the assignment meeting; there really are "no stupid questions," and you'll show respect for the external client by seeking to be efficient in resolving the obvious issues up front. Before leaving, be sure to ask when the assignment is due, and when before that time the assigning attorney wants you to check back with a preliminary report. Finally, tell the assigning attorney, "I'm sure I'll have additional questions as I get underway; what's the best time and way to reach you for clarification or guidance?"

In all of the foregoing behaviors—each of which is its own, self-contained little rule of etiquette—you'll convey the earnestness that says to a more senior attorney, "This person is on the ball; I'm in good hands."

"Do You Have a Second?"

So, now it's a day or two later, and you're in the heart of the assignment, when suddenly you hit a brick wall; you need guidance in order to go on. Trotting down to the assigning attorney's office, you find a scene of loosely organized madness; a secretary is putting one caller on hold while the second line rings, there's a fresh six-inch stack of papers in the "in" box, hand-marked documents are strewn across the assigner's desk in various stages of completion, and the assigning attorney is hunched over a keyboard, tapping out an email and clearly enrapt in so doing.

In other words, you arrive *in medias res*; you're about to interrupt. You're about to take the assigning attorney out of what he or she was doing—out of the frame of mind, thought process, and state of knowledge being enjoyed before you arrived—and ask the attorney to shift gears in order to reenter your project, get up to speed on where you started and where you are now, understand the obstacle you're facing, and help guide you forward; in short, to switch gears completely, and at high speed.

Consider, instead, asking the secretary how you can secure a moment of the assigning attorney's time, to help resolve an issue in your project; alternatively, consider emailing or instant messaging the more senior attorney to see if and when they are free to meet. That gives the assigner the chance to resolve any crises in an orderly fashion, and thus devote more complete and thoughtful attention to yours. You'll likely get a clearer, more helpful response, while at the same time not adding to the pressures on the more senior attorney. (Of course, if you're truly in meltdown mode, or up against a critical deadline, then interruption may be appropriate.)

The rule of etiquette here is not to presume that your own issue takes precedence, but to defer where possible to the more senior attorneys to prioritize the challenges they face—including the challenges you face on their behalf—in the way that most efficiently and effectively serves their external clients.

"Mr. Corleone Insists . . . "

What happens when the conclusion you reach appears to be different than the one that the assigning attorney expected? That happens; after all, if all of the answers were known or preordained, there would be no real reason to occupy you with finding them anew. Still, it can be disturbing, even terrifying, to feel as though you're about to deliver a different answer than was anticipated. What if you've uncovered something that causes a whole case or deal to move into uncharted territory? Worse yet, what if you're wrong? It's enough to make you want to sit in your office with the door closed, either staring at the phone or updating your résumé, and many a junior attorney does just that.

In the classic film *The Godfather*, the Don's *consigliere*, attorney Tom Hagen, tells someone who has failed to accede to the Don's wishes that "Mr. Corleone is a man who insists on hearing bad news immediately." Similarly, your rule of etiquette when you have bad news to deliver should be to do so immediately, and preferably in person. This is an instance where interruption is appropriate; moreover, it's one in which your ability to look the assigner in the eye and lay out your case can be critical in conveying the importance of what you have to say, and helping the assigning attorney to access both your verbal and non-verbal cues in order to integrate the news and decide how to proceed.

At the very least, convey your conclusion by phone, if a face-to-face meeting isn't possible for some reason. Try to stay away from voicemail messages of bad news, and avoid email except as a last resort; as a communication medium, email lacks the ability to convey tone and nuance, and is thus uncommonly prone to misunderstanding at a time when concision and content are key.

"Better Late Than Never . . . NOT!"

A handy guideline for both assigning attorneys and those who work for them, is that everything takes longer than you think it will. When an assigning attorney says, "This should take you an hour or two," plan for more like four or six; if you finish early, then more's the better. (Note, though, that this is different from an assigning attorney saying, "Spend an hour on this and then report back." In that case, an hour means an hour, either because there's a looming deadline or due to a budget consideration—or both—and you should adhere to the restriction.)

Still, sometimes work really does expand beyond the time available for its completion, and against your best efforts you find that you're about to run late, or worse yet, you actually blow clean past the deadline. Many junior attorneys are tempted to conclude that, "If they aren't screaming for it, then they must not need it," and to keep working—or just hide—until the project is finally done, or escape is impossible.

The rule of etiquette in this situation, however, is precisely the opposite: As soon as you perceive that a deadline won't be met, inform the supervising attorney immediately, and work out a new timeline. Hiding under your desk with a blanket, a flashlight, and a three-day supply of crackers will avail you not in these circumstances. While you're busy assuming that the assigning attorney really didn't need this when she said she did, she's busy assuming that you have it all taken care of, and what falls through the gap between those two assumptions is the interest of the external client, who may be prejudiced (or simply annoyed) by not receiving an answer when he wanted it. Scrambling to get a project back on track in such circumstances often leads to mistakes, and at the very least leaves a poor impression of your performance, when your substantive work is actually solid. Avoid both the risk and the perception of error with timely communication.

"Whose (Dead)Line Is It Anyway?"

Related to the rule of timeliness is its corollary, which comes into play in the seemingly miraculous circumstances where a deadline has been extended. Imagine that a client has told the supervising attorney that they need the answer to a thorny legal question by the end of the day on Friday, and that the supervising attorney has thus set a deadline for you of close-of-business on Thursday, to allow for time to review and revise your work. Then, unexpectedly, the client calls to say, "As it turns out, our timing has slipped, and I really don't need your answer until Monday." This is the lawyer's equivalent of a stay of execution;

vast vistas of additional time to complete the assignment open before you.

Right?

Wrong. Just because the final delivery time has changed, doesn't mean that your expected delivery time has changed, nor should it. Specifically, just because you perceive that more time is available overall to complete the assignment does not mean that the additional time accrues solely to your personal benefit. The assigning attorney may have his or her own conflicting demands, be they professional or personal, so that the additional time may not actually help much. If you appropriate that time to yourself, then you may be creating a greater logjam at the new time of delivery than would have been the case if nothing had changed at all.

The rule of etiquette here is to communicate with the supervising attorney about how—if at all—the additional time will be allocated between you. Start with the assumption that nothing has changed in terms of your own due date, regardless of the change in the overall delivery date; that gives the supervising attorney the chance to fit your work most effectively into both the timeline for that specific project and the overall demands on his or her time. Plus, it creates the opportunity to exceed the client's expectations; just because the client says that the lawyers have more time, doesn't mean that the lawyers have to take it. Many times, delivering something in less time than expected can create a strong positive impression of efficiency and cost-effectiveness, as well as of putting the client first. Don't fail to perceive an opportunity to impress both internal and external clients.

"Is Anybody Out There?"

Let's shift our scene somewhat, and enter the office of the more senior attorney. Amid the tumult of her day, a thought comes into her mind of the more junior colleague, toiling away on a project assigned to him earlier, and the thought is one that requires outreach—perhaps a status check, possibly the disclosure of a new fact that might be of help to the more junior attorney, maybe a notice of change in the timetable for completion. The senior attorney sends a message, by email or voicemail, and receives back . . . nothing. No acknowledgment of receipt, no reply, just the sound of one hand clapping, and that hand is not attached to the arm of the more junior colleague.

What do you do when a more senior attorney (or anyone, for that matter, from the partner in charge to the peanut vendor) reaches out for you? The rule of etiquette is, "respond." A simple "got it" will serve, in many circumstances. When an attorney leading a project communicates with you as a team member, he's creating in his head a mental checklist item; by acknowledging the communication, and if possible reporting the status, you allow the supervisor to tick off that item and move on to the next, thereby keeping the entire project on track. Silence here is not golden, it's merely unhelpful.

Now, sometimes this notion of constantly responding can get a little bit out of hand. We know of one eager young attorney who has a habit of responding to everything, including ordinary course responses to their own responses. Before long, a twenty-layer German chocolate cake of nested emails tells the tale of the attorney's own commitment to always have the last word: a "thanks" sent to them comes back as "no problem," followed by "happy to help," "glad we're on track," "have a good weekend," "take care," etc. (but without the benefit of tasty icing between the layers). One client of our acquaintance makes this particular attorney's dedication to have the last word into something of a game; the client keeps responding, just to see how long the attorney can string this all out. So, apply a rule of reason here; you should by all means acknowledge receipt of a substantive email, but please bring down the curtain on the Alphonse and Gaston show after a single act.

"Where's Waldo?"

Staying with our theme of the more senior attorney searching out the more junior colleague, hardly anything can be more frustrating to a project leader than being unable to locate a team member when needed. This doesn't mean that you need to chain yourself to your desk, or take your phone to bed with you, but it does mean that you need to be capable of being located when you're most likely to be needed. The rule of etiquette, then, is to let someone know how to reach you when you're away from your desk during normal business hours, or outside that period when circumstances are such that you would be expected to be reachable.

If you're going to lunch, tell your secretary, and give a sense of when you expect to be back; if you'll be in a meeting, let your assistant know whether you can be disturbed, and if so then for whom you *must* be disturbed; if you will be in the bathroom, washing your feet in the sink (a true story, but one for another chapter, or perhaps another book altogether), then either return quickly or leave a trail of bread crumbs so that you can be found in a pinch. In all events, accept that you're a part of a collaborative effort—and a key part, no matter how junior you may think you are—and accord your teammates the courtesy of being able to be located when required.

"Check, Please"

No, this does not refer to the etiquette of picking up the tab (we deal with dining elsewhere). Rather, we are thinking here about the need to check your own email with some reasonable frequency. When you are "on the clock," during normal business hours, you really ought to check your email regularly. How regularly? Well, as in all things, a rule of reason applies; once a day is too little, and once a minute is too much. Think of the context of your own workday, and plan accordingly. Do you have three depositions lined up to defend that day? If so, then checking between them is probably the best that you can do. Are you in a multi-hour in-person negotiation? If so, then it may be hard to check other than at a break. But if you are sitting at your desk, dealing with the ordinary course of the day's work, then (sadly) you should recognize that, increasingly, clients internal and external expect you to respond promptly—certainly within the hour, probably within far less than that, and amazingly often, almost instantly.

What with the way that the workday has expanded in our profession, and with the ubiquity of technology, a not dissimilar rule applies even after hours. Plan to check and respond where, when, and as soon as possible. We recognize that this can go seriously awry, very quickly; no one wants to be sitting at a family dinner or a little league game with the person who can't put away their smartphone, and the etiquette of being present, attentive, and respectful should serve as a check on letting your work obligations obliterate all aspects of your personal life. Still, it would be equally unreasonable, in today's world, to leave the office at 5:00 on most days and assume that you don't have to be accessible before 9:00 the following morning; too much happens after ordinary business hours, and whether you like it or not, people are depending upon you, or are hoping to. In the final analysis, law is a service profession, and to serve you have to be able to be reached.

During those times, whether throughout the workday or outside normal business hours, when you know you will simply be unreachable for whatever reason, set an "out-of-office" message on your email. That way, you can at least let those who are seeking you out know that it may be a while until you get back to them, whether because you are traveling or because you are in court. Clients may be slightly frustrated by your unavailability (and often more than slightly so), but at least no one will feel ignored by you.

"Can You Hear Me Now?"

Speaking of being unreachable, one surprising workplace development in recent years has been the increasing use of MP3 players, noise-cancellin headphones, and earbuds in the office. It is not uncommon, especially during the summer associate months, to walk by offices where the occupant is plugged in and working away, literally tuned out from their surroundings. We are willing to concede that each of us thrives in our own unique work environment, and sometimes it is no doubt best to be able to shut out the world and focus. Still, there is something somewhat off-putting about a colleague who seems to be present—his door is open, his light is on, he is at his desk—but who has no idea that you are there until you start waving frantically or shouting over his musical soundtrack or white-noise generator. If you must tune out, then consider at least closing your door; many times, that alone will create the environment you need in order to be productive, while still allowing for the possibility of you hearing someone's knock.

When to Hit "Send"

We have already written extensively, in this chapter and elsewhere, about the expansion of work to fill the time allotted for its completion, and the way in which both economics and technology have combined to make the practice of law a 24/7 profession; no rule of etiquette will take us back to a quieter, more humanely-paced time. Still, you might consider whether the fact that you are working all the time requires you to send emails at all hours of the day and night and over the weekend. Instead, think about whether all weekend and late-night emails are created equal. When a client is waiting for a document to review, or opposing counsel on a deal is hammering you for the next turn of an agreement, then of course you will want to respond as soon as you can, no matter what the day or hour. But when the email is something less critical, think about whether it is more likely to fall off the radar screen if it is sent outside business hours. One of our respected friends and colleagues makes a point of drafting such lower-priority emails whenever convenient for them—even at 2:00 on Sunday morning—but then saving them in their "draft" folder and only sending them after 8:30 or 9:00 on Monday morning. An email sent during normal business hours is often easier for the recipient to deal with and respond to immediately than one that is sent at an unexpected time. Moreover, what could be more polite than saving your addressee from having to spend even a moment of their Sunday afternoon registering and acknowledging your choice of the vegetarian entrée for the monthly practice group lunch? Many matters are urgent, but not all; we would encourage you to make the world a more sane place by considering the time when sending emails.

Chapter Three

Office Etiquette: Working With Peers

Work colleagues who are your peers are especially important to your career development. You will be traveling the same path with these people, moving forward in your careers together. Some lawyers will view their peers as their competition. Resist the temptation to view your professional life through the lens of scarcity; it is not just possible for peers to succeed together, but in today's team-oriented and collaborative work environment, it's essential if we are all to achieve the goal of making the total pie of work and reward larger.

Thus, focus on developing collegial relationships with your peers, notwithstanding your knowledge that the future is uncertain. Assume the attitude that you are part of a collective enterprise and everyone's success inures to the benefit of the firm. Moreover, lawyers move between firms with regularity, go into business for themselves, find positions in-house, or leave the profession entirely. Your work colleague today may be your client or your boss tomorrow.

Since we cannot know what the future holds, treat all of your peers with the respect and collegiality they deserve. By demonstrating simple kindness and respect for your colleagues, you elevate yourself and—at the same time—will create a reputation for kindness and decency that will extend beyond your time and immediate circle of contacts at a particular firm.

The following are some suggestions for success in the workplace when working with peers:

Avoid the Gossip Mill

There's a difference between gossip and intelligence-gathering. While it's important to understand the intricacies of office politics and have a nuanced knowledge of who's good to work for and who might better be avoided if possible, draw a bright line at idle gossip and avoid it whenever possible. One can say it's simply good manners not to talk about people behind their backs; you would not want people doing the same with you as the subject, so why engage in that type of behavior? You do not want to have a reputation among your peers as someone who is untrustworthy or indiscreet.

On the other hand, gathering information about law firm news—who may be a good mentor (or an indifferent mentor) and so forth—is an acceptable and, some would say, important skill to acquire. Know the difference between information-gathering and gossip and be scrupulous about not engaging in hurtful chatter, whether in person or online.

Share Information

Create a mutually supportive environment among your peer group by passing on information. For example, if you are aware of an upcoming continuing legal education class on a subject of interest or the opportunity to speak at a professional seminar, share that information with your peers. Creating a flow of information to others will help ensure that similar information will flow in your direction.

Create a Network

As you advance in your career, create a network of colleagues and become a referral source for information and ideas. Rather than hording names of potential client contacts, work together to build business and share expertise. You may specialize in labor and employment law, but you need a trustworthy peer who specializes in tax law in order to attract clients. The process of building silos between your firm's practice areas and peers will not benefit you or your firm in the long run. Be the person who creates the connections within your firm and beyond. Not only will your connectivity create value for your firm but it will also benefit your clients.

In our experience, the need to create a personal network is the single most difficult piece of career development advice for associates to embrace. Most lawyers have come to the profession with a focus on its intellectual aspects, and with a long and proud history of academic success as a condition precedent; they think of themselves as smart, and they think of their intelligence and learning as the reasons why they will be sought out as counselors. No doubt, the intellectual element of law is essential, but it is also assumed; clients both internal and external are generally unlikely to select you for your brilliance, but are likely instead simply to expect it. Rather, the way that work is secured, and that careers are made, is through ever-expanding and maturing networks of interpersonal connections. The personal bond that you establish with a supervising attorney—through many of the polite behaviors we describe herein—leads them to wish to work with you again; the similar bonds you establish with your peers lead you all to continue to work together even after some (perhaps including you) have left your firm, or even left the law completely. The contacts you made in college, or playing sports in your free time, or walking your dog in the morning, become your clients, or you become theirs. Human beings are social animals, and while we hope never to lose the meritocratic aspects of our society that create meaningful opportunities for social mobility, we also should recognize that the lawyer-client relationship is a relationship of trust, and trust only happens when people know one another.

All that being said, you will not want to pursue the creation of a personal network as a thing unto itself; "networking" is not a competitive pursuit, nor is it one that stands apart from the living, breathing human beings in the network. We would encourage you instead to look at creating a personal network the same way that you would look at creating a community; grow relationships with people you know, like, and trust, and with whom you want to enjoy a long-term connection. One of David's partners describes good networking as being like dating: You will go on lots of "first dates," but limit your "second dates" to the smaller group with whom you hit it off. Then develop the discipline of following up regularly and building a lasting connection over time. Finally, we would urge you to not do so primarily and cynically to get work—the work will come when the relationships are strong—but instead to do so because along that path lies the meaningful and rewarding life.

Communicate Carefully

When drafting or forwarding emails at the office, be sure to exercise caution before you hit "send." Many a relationship and reputation has been tarnished, sometimes beyond repair, by a thoughtless email, an equally tactless forwarding of an email, a tawdry tweet, or a reckless blog entry. Avoid denigrating colleagues, belittling others in correspondence, or otherwise behaving in a fashion that would cause you grief later.

Once you have committed words to email or other electronic means, assume that they will be forwarded and seen by everyone in the world.

An excellent resource for lawyers to consult regarding email etiquette is *Send: The Essential Guide to Email for Office and Home* by David Shipley and Will Schwalbe, which we highly recommend.

Recognize Life-Cycle Events

When your peers get married, have children, or experience a loss, acknowledge these life-cycle events in a timely manner. This can be as simple as an email (although this may be a bit impersonal in some instances) or, ideally, a personal, handwritten note or greeting card.

Sending a greeting card to a colleague's home is a thoughtful way to show support for another person. Keep a variety of greeting cards or personal stationery in your office, along with stamps, so that it's easy to jot a note and send it when you hear news. *Just a Note to Say . . . The Perfect Words for Every Occasion* by Florence Isaacs offers excellent advice to help you draft meaningful notes. What you write does not have to be profound or perfect, or even very long; two or three lines will often suffice. Simply put some sincere thoughts to paper and send it as soon as possible.

Some major life-cycle events worthy of recognition are:

Weddings

When you are invited to a colleague's wedding, respond to the invitation in a timely manner. Buy an appropriate present; if the couple is registered at a store, consider buying a gift from the wedding registry. Otherwise, money is always an appropriate wedding gift. Check with someone whose judgment you trust if you are unsure of the appropriate amount.

Births and Adoptions

When a coworker or colleague announces the birth or adoption of a child, take a moment and acknowledge this milestone with a card or small gift. A few words of welcome are always appreciated. When considering a small gift, you need not spend a great deal of money. Many stores carry small items, or you can order a personalized piggybank or bib online. While gift giving is not required, it can be a kind gesture.

Deaths

When someone in your office experiences a death in his or her immediate family, good manners dictate that you acknowledge your colleague's loss. Send a sympathy card as soon as possible with a personal note. Keep a supply of sympathy cards on hand or write a personal note on stationery.

In addition to sending a sympathy card, consider visiting in person to show support and respect for your colleague. Whether you attend the viewing, wake, or funeral, or pay a shiva visit, taking the time to personally acknowledge another's loss is simply good manners. If you are unsure about religious customs for any life-cycle event, find some-one to ask. Do not forgo the opportunity to do the right thing because you're uncertain about what to do at a wake. Ask and show up.

If you are close to a colleague, it is appropriate to make a donation to the charity of the family's choice to honor the memory of the deceased. Typically, information about charitable donations is noted in the obituary announce-ment or available at the funeral home.

The Etiquette of Sharing Office Space

Once upon a time, not only did many lawyers have their own private office from the outset, but in fact that office might have had its own secretarial office as a gateway. Today, though, with space at a premium, lawyers are increasingly being asked to share space, especially at the outset of their careers. In the future, as our ability to work remotely increases, the dedicated single-lawyer office may become a thing of the past, as lawyers "hotel" in firms during the times when they need to be physically present on-site. How should you approach the issue of shared office space?

As it happens, we are writing this particular section a mere forty-eight hours after dropping our son off for his freshman year of college; his dorm room, to be shared for the next nine months or so with a roommate, is a pretty cozy space, to say the least (or perhaps the most). In thinking about shared office space, think about the best aspects of other shared space experiences you may have had, whether at school or at home; the keys to success are patience, politeness, and respect. Taking the alpha-animal approach and exerting dominion over your realm might work for you, but it is unlikely to work for both you and your officemate alike; instead, seek to cooperate, avoid needless noise and mess, and try to respect one another's needs as best you can under the circumstances.

As in all things (and as we find ourselves continuously reminding throughout this text), communication is essential; if you need privacy for a personal phone call or a tense negotiation, or just to write a thorny legal memo, let your officemate know in advance, and work out who will get the space for the time in question. Remember that conference rooms and workspaces can serve as temporary offices to relieve the pressure of living on top of one another. Finally, look at the bright side: By assigning you to a shared space, your firm may have taken the first step along the path of helping you to build your personal network.

The Etiquette of Business Travel

So much can be said about the rules of etiquette as rules of the road, but what about rules of etiquette for when you are on the road? Truthfully, a whole book could be written on this topic alone. Fortunately, the book you are reading already covers most of what you will need, whether in terms of working with colleagues at the same and different levels of the work world hierarchy, or dealing with issues of social etiquette, or approaching questions of client interactions or client development. Our many rules of the road work on the road, as well.

A few points call out for separate attention when out and about, however. First among these is the importance of discretion. Whether you are traveling in a plane or on a train, or even on the elevator from your office to the lobby of your building, you should be aware at all times that you are in a public place. What you say can and will be heard, so be discreet. As a lawyer, you have an ethical duty to maintain client confidences, and you may be subject to other duties not to disclose non-public information; remembering that you are not alone when you are not alone can help you to live up to those duties.

David was once on a train from New York to Philadelphia, where two associates from another firm were sitting across the aisle. How did he know that they were associates from another firm? Because they were talking loudly, over the noise of the train, about where they worked, with whom they worked, against whom they worked, and on what they were working. It didn't take long to know an awful lot about them, and about many others with whom they were interacting. Finally, when the discussion seemed about to turn explicitly personal and likely unpleasantly so, David intervened (gently) to remind them that about half of the people on that train were lawyers, and the rest were probably clients, so that it might be better to delay the conversation until later.

Another key point of etiquette while traveling is remembering that the rules—of etiquette, and of everything else—are not suspended while you are away. This applies especially to things such as expenses and activities; if you wouldn't do it or expense it at home, then don't do so on the road. This rule goes for things such as minibar charges, in-room movies, lavish dining, and other entertainments. If you are away on business, then you are away specifically on business; focus on the work while you are at work (and while you are away, assume that you are basically always at work), and leave the pleasure for personal time. This is not to say that all travel must be a slog, but merely to remind you that, in the cold fluorescent light of the office of a supervising attorney reviewing your expenses—or worse yet, of a client reviewing the bill—activities and charges that seem reasonable or justified (perhaps you are thinking of them as "combat pay") will look very much different.

Chapter Four

Office Etiquette: Working With Those More Junior

The milieu of the senior attorney working with the more junior lawyer is not merely the flip side of that of the supervised working with the supervisor. While both are working to serve their common external client, the more junior is not the "client" of the more senior in the same way that the senior is the client of the junior. A different relationship of obligation exists between the senior and the junior that is in many ways more important than even a client-counselor relationship.

More senior attorneys have in their care the career development of their junior colleagues, as lawyers and as future leaders; as a result, the rules of etiquette that frame their interactions have special consequence. Senior attorneys should conduct their interactions with junior team members so as to obtain not only the best work in the short term, but also the most growth in the long run.

This is true even when it appears unlikely that a junior colleague will stay associated with the work environment for many years, as some of the best potential clients are former colleagues.

How does the relationship between supervisor and supervised attorney play itself out in some specific situations? Let's go to the tape (does anyone say that anymore?) with the following observations and suggestions for fostering impeccable etiquette in the workplace:

"Praise Publicly, Criticize Privately"

Into each life, a little rain must fall, and into each work relationship, a little constructive (hopefully) criticism is all but equally inevitable. When you as the senior attorney have such feedback to provide to the junior lawyer, how you do so is at least as important as what you say.

Attorneys are notoriously focused on the task at hand, and in so focusing can lose track of where they are and what's going on around them, sometimes quite literally. This can lead to criticism being provided loudly with the door open, in a crowded hallway, on the elevator, in the building lobby, or even at a meeting in front of clients, counterparties, and opposing counsel. Such public displays of criticism are thoughtless at best, and destructive at worst; they violate the cardinal rule of etiquette in this circumstance, which is, "praise publicly, criticize privately."

Public comments about performance should consist exclusively of genuine expressions of praise; a "great job!" delivered in front of other lawyers and staff members can buoy not only the spirits of the person to whom the accolade is directed, but also the morale of the entire office. People want to work in a place where their contributions are noticed and valued; as a leader—whether of a project or an office or an entire firm—you have it in your treasury to dispense public praise as your coin of the realm, and you should do so whenever the performance merits it.

By contrast, criticism should only be delivered privately, behind a closed door, and in a voice that won't be overheard. Nothing chills the office more than being able to tell that "so-and-so's being taken to the wood shed," because you can hear the screaming coming from the corner office. Moreover, wherever possible, criticism should be delivered in person, and not by email or voicemail.

Nobody likes conflict, and the temptation to avoid it by launching an electronic missile at a subordinate is sometimes almost irresistible, but resist you should. Errant subordinates deserve your engagement and interaction if they are to learn from their missteps, and, frankly, they are entitled to the respect of a face-to-face meeting. In fact, if the temptation to avoid an in-person meeting is all but overwhelming, that's almost certainly an indication that meeting in person is precisely what the etiquette of the critique truly requires.

"Be the Driver, Not the Whip"

Related to the notion of public praise and private criticism is a stylistic point on leadership, which has an attached component of etiquette. We must each find our own management voice, and many a text on leadership can present as many convincing arguments against the "buddy" style of leadership as against the "cruel taskmaster" model. No matter what voice turns out to be your own, though, the etiquette of leadership suggests that you should focus on the goal and on guiding your team toward its attainment; *ad hominem* attacks and personal invective are unlikely to get you to your destination. In all of your interactions, seek to treat everyone—most especially subordinates—with the respect and human decency that they deserve. Even the harshest boss will be perceived as fair if she focuses her efforts properly.

"Watch the Clock . . . and Don't Be Late!"

Every senior team member becomes subject to competing demands on his or her time. Meetings bump against
meetings; conference calls against client calls; professional
obligations against personal ones. Scheduling—especially in
an increasingly 24/7, instant-gratification world—becomes
a nightmare (one that a healthy relationship with a competent secretary can do wonders to ease), and keeping on
time and on task seems all but impossible.

Nonetheless, senior lawyers have a special responsibility
to make every effort to be on time for their obligations;
promptness is a point of etiquette and a matter of respect
for the time of others. All lawyers live in fear of being late
for a court appearance or a filing deadline, and most dread
being late for a client obligation; yet many are perfectly
willing to be late for—or completely miss—office partner
meetings, meetings with non-lawyer staff, and the like.

Sometimes unanticipated client demands do interfere
in ways that simply cannot be avoided, and of course the
clients are paying to keep the lights on. Barring such true
emergencies, though, the senior lawyer should make every
possible effort to arrive for meetings on time, stay until they
end, and forswear interruptions such as cell phone calls.
On the subject of personal electronic devices, try to make
every effort not to brandish phones publicly or to scroll

for messages idly. It is far better to arrive on time and ask for a short break for an electronics check (perhaps coupled with a "bio break") than to keep everyone waiting or to divide your attention during the meeting.

When other demands of a less-than-urgent nature are allowed to take precedence, the clear message to everyone else in the meeting is, "My time is more important than yours." This is hardly a way to get the best out of everyone, or make the most productive use of collaboration opportunities. Instead, an in-progress meeting may stop to admit a latecomer, who then must be caught up on what transpired before, or may stop when a key participant walks out, bringing all progress to a halt before responsibilities can be allocated and deliverables set. Make it your goal to show up on time, stay throughout, and leave in an orderly fashion, so that all of the participants can benefit from your wisdom and insight.

"Give Us the Tools, and We Will Finish the Job"

Survey after survey shows that junior lawyers crave two things: responsibility and feedback. We've spoken above about the etiquette of constructive criticism, but what can etiquette tell us about assigning responsibility? Simply this: To the extent appropriate, try to approach supervisory situations in a way that makes each member of the team feel that they have something to accomplish and for which they are accountable. Provide clear direction, set concrete objectives, and require continuous reporting of progress, but where possible allow the workers to perform the work themselves.

For example, consider planning in advance, to the extent possible, to break a project down into several component parts, and then figure out which ones can be further broken out for some separate and independent work. It's typical, for instance, in the context of a large M&A project, for the most junior lawyers to be tasked with due diligence and document review projects, but there are always smaller ancillary agreements to be drafted, which conform reasonably closely to established precedent forms, but which nonetheless require both customization and negotiation; consider letting the more junior associate who prepared the first draft stay with the project to negotiate the changes with their counterpart on the other side of the table (subject of course to your review and client sign-off). Even a limited opportunity to stretch will almost certainly be met with eagerness and attention to detail that exceeds your expectations. Remember, we all start somewhere, and that somewhere is from square one.

"Success Has a Thousand Fathers, but Failure Is an Orphan"

In the context of etiquette, perhaps this should be rephrased as, "Success has a thousand children." Many have been credited with the phrase, "There is no limit to what we can accomplish, so long as we don't care who gets the credit." The etiquette of supervision suggests that credit should be shared broadly, and not sparingly. Everyone likes to bask in the reflected glow of success; graciousness compels us to cause the glow to shine as brightly as we can, and to illuminate the lives of as many members of the team as possible.

Then again, sometimes things don't turn out quite as well as we had hoped. When that happens, a sober examination of what went wrong and to whom the failure can be traced is critical to avoiding the same or similar mistakes in the future; that inquiry, though, and most especially its outcome, should take place quietly and without public expressions of blame or reproach wherever possible.

It may not always be practicable for the senior attorney to avoid identifying the source of an error, but the etiquette of leadership amid failure strongly suggests that the right thing to do is to acknowledge the failure and the leadership, and to foster the notion that "the buck stops here." Taking responsibility—and even blame—for the errors of those you supervise can be hard and painful. When done correctly, though, and within the context of a healthy team, it can also build loyalty and a sense of obligation not to let the same thing happen again.

"Thank You"

Just as credit should be shared as broadly as is warranted, so should gratitude. Every child learns that "please" and "thank you" are the two critical phrases of rudimentary etiquette; it's thus shocking how many adults forget those phrases—most especially "thank you"—in their everyday lives.

Expressions of thanks go even further when made to more junior team members; they acknowledge service and sacrifice, and thus make service and sacrifice more meaningful and rewarding.

Nearly everyone has had a project come in late in the day, or had a piece of work expand to require a late night effort or a weekend trip into the office. One of the burdens that often falls upon more junior lawyers is to stay late or work the weekend at the behest of the more senior practitioner, so that something can be "on my desk first thing in the morning" or "ready to roll on Monday," yet too few of the senior lawyers who benefit from such hard work remember to say, "Thanks for staying late," or "I really appreciate you getting this done over the weekend." Proper etiquette requires of the supervisor an expression of gratitude for the effort of the subordinate. Just say "thanks."

Thanks are great, but sometimes something a bit more significant may be in order. Periodically, those under your supervision go far above and beyond expectations. Yes, if you and they are fortunate, then they are being compensated well for their efforts, and yes, if you and they are even more fortunate, then there may be some additional compensation or recognition at year-end, but little is as effective to say thank you for an extra effort as an immediate, special recognition. A gift certificate for a nice dinner, or a pair of tickets to a show or a game, or even just taking the team out for a drink or a snack after work can do the trick. Don't be held prisoner by what you can expense, but instead let your own personal generosity, within the confines of your own reasonable financial wherewithal and budget, be your guide; your gratitude and consideration will likely be repaid many times over.

Chapter Five

Office Etiquette:
Working With Staff

The question of the etiquette of working with staff may be the thorniest one presented in this book, bound up as it is with issues of class (the great unmentionable in American society), seniority, even gender. Moreover, it's an issue that cuts across generations, as the most senior attorneys may well have been brought up in an age and a culture where relationships with staff were dramatically different than they are today, while the newest attorneys may never have worked in an environment where they have been asked to supervise anyone else, and may be utterly clueless as how best to do so. Play all of this against the backdrop of legal liability for harassment and other workplace misbehaviors, and you are looking at a veritable minefield for the unprepared.

In the not-so-distant past, etiquette and custom both compelled a certain type of order on lawyer-staff relations.

The lawyer was able to take on a decidedly superior role, whether of lord and master or of benevolent dictator, while staff was able to feel some reflected benefit of being associated with respected professionals and performing valued, integral roles within the lawyer's world. After all, most lawyers didn't type their own briefs or their own contracts, weren't easily accessible outside business hours or without the intermediation of a secretary, and generally did not function alone in the professional world; a trusted staff member was basically always at hand.

Today, of course, the world has been turned upside down. No matter how hard the eldest generation of lawyers claims to have worked in their youth, study after study finds that work has expanded to fill the time allotted for its completion, and that the time so allotted has expanded to encompass all twenty-four hours of the day and all seven days of the week. Since staff working hours have by and large not changed (save for the advent of the 'round-the-clock resource support center), this means that a large portion of a lawyer's work life will be spent working alone, or at the least without a secretary handy.

Moreover, law school graduates today arrive with years of computer experience behind them; many feel, if anything, more comfortable processing their own work than they do relying upon anyone else to do so for them. Finally, they are arriving at the doorstep of a system where the traditional roles of all of the parties are completely up for grabs; more senior attorneys can no longer guide them by saying, "When I was just a young whippersnapper . . . ," and more tenured staff members are often fearful that their relevance is on the wane. Into that volatile mix come junior lawyers who may feel that they need to assert themselves and their authority in order to be respected.

What can etiquette teach us to guide us through such turbulent waters? Beyond the many employment-law-mandated requirements we could cite, here are five helpful rules to bear in mind for working with staff effectively:

"The Name of the Game Is . . . "

If one key to successful networking is remembering names (see "name amnesia" in chapter nine), then one equally valuable tip for successful interaction with staff is to learn and remember with whom you're working. These aren't merely helpers; these are your colleagues and teammates. Imagine the manager of a baseball team not knowing his players' names and filling in the line-up card using numbers alone; that's not the sort of manager who will lead his team to the World Series by motivating everyone to come together as one unit.

Establishing a personal connection by simply knowing and remembering staff members' names will go farther than you can imagine to build the sort of respectful environment that breeds success and service; staff members will feel engaged, and not merely commanded, and you'll feel responsible for them as people, and not simply a consumer of their efforts. Knowing with whom you're working is the touchstone of polite and respectful behavior in the workplace.

Early in David's career, when he was working as the most junior lawyer on a securities offering, he was spending many late nights at the office with the rest of the team, drafting and revising a registration statement and prospectus. Inevitably in those days before email, the end of each evening's work would be a mad scramble to photocopy a new draft and stuff it in envelopes for overnight delivery to the other members of the working group. (To this day, twenty-five years later, David can remember the pick-up times for the succession of delivery services that would take those mailings, at successively higher costs as the times grew later in the evening.) One mid-level associate with whom David worked (who is now the general counsel of a major multinational corporation) had a miraculous touch with the support staff; it seemed that everyone wanted to stay a little bit later and help him out. When asked how he did it, the mid-level said, "I just know everyone on the staff; my wife jokes that at the holiday party, none of the lawyers know me as well as the folks in the mailroom." While there was a bit of hyperbole there, the fundamental lesson should not be lost; it takes an enormous effort to make anything happen in our legal system or in our modern business environment, and everyone at every level counts.

Get Over Yourself

Respect is earned, not compelled; to earn it, approach staff with some semblance of humility. Whether you've been practicing law for forty years or for forty-five minutes, the practice of law is what you do, not who you are, and those around you—from the managing partner to the messenger and back again—have something to teach you.

Humility does not imply supplication, nor does it compel you to be everyone's buddy; nonetheless, open your mind to the notion that those around you have their own areas of experience and expertise, and accord them the deference in those areas that is their due.

Unless you've been working as a secretary in your spare time, your secretary knows more about word processing than you do now, or ever will; find a way to pass your work through him or her, in order to polish it to its highest luster.

Your secretary also knows more about how to manage a database of contacts and a calendar of obligations than you ever will; consolidate both activities in his or her hands.

The people who run the copy center know more about making copies and binding sets of documents than you will ever care to know; the information technology people know more about your IT systems than you can imagine; the facilities staff knows more about how to set up a conference than you ever dreamed possible. Draw on his or her expertise by treating everyone with respect.

David, in particular, has been blessed with exceptional support from exceptional staff over the years, from the extraordinary secretary who taught him how to run his practice as a partner, to the phenomenal paralegal who knows more about the internal workings of his clients' legal departments and corporate structures than anyone on the planet. Every now and again, a new associate on his team will chafe a bit at the notion of a paralegal or a secretary telling him or her that the way to handle this or that situation with a client's internal procedures is as follows; the word will filter back to David that the associate's attitude is one of, "Who does that paralegal think they are? I'm a lawyer!" Regardless of who the paralegal or the secretary may think they are, David knows precisely who they are, which is someone irreplaceable and priceless;

after hearing of any such attitude, David also has a pretty good sense of who the associate is, too, which is someone who has an enormous amount to learn.

Nothing Is Beneath You

We've highlighted the importance of relying upon the expertise of staff, but we'd recommend not doing so to the point of personal paralysis. Because the work has now slipped the bounds of the working day, the time will come when you need to make a photocopy or send a fax late at night or on the weekend, when there's nobody around to help you. Ask appropriate staff members to teach you the basics of what you need to know in order to function independently under such circumstances; doing so will not only engender their respect for you as a fully functioning member of the team, but will also inspire within you a greater appreciation for what your colleagues do for you.

We've seen time after time the example of a lawyer who is respected by the staff as a pitch-in player motivating staff members to want to pitch in as well. Making common effort in service of the common cause is a positive rule of etiquette and of leadership. When you're running around like a chicken with its head cut off with ten minutes to go before the wire transfer deadline for a closing, relying upon your support staff to have gotten all of the documents and signature pages collated and checked, you'll learn how much it matters to them and to the goal of client service that you are leading by example.

Recognize Contributions

Finally, recognize staff in particular for their contributions to the team effort. When a case is won, or a deal closes, too often the kudos is conferred only on the lawyers, and all too frequently are the vital support staff overlooked. Doing so reinforces the notion among support staff that the lawyer-staff divide is the line between two castes; staff can easily question why they are working so hard, and so loyally, for such ungrateful employers.

By contrast, we know of lawyers who routinely single out staff members for public praise and appreciation, and who receive in return a level of hard work and loyalty that transcends anything that mere money can buy. The rule of etiquette known as "politeness" applies here; spread praise broadly, and by all means include the staff within the ambit of your public expressions of gratitude.

Acknowledge Staff Milestones and Celebrations

Beyond knowing the staff, appreciating their skills and expertise, and recognizing their contributions, be sure to acknowledge their milestones and celebrations. In today's world, where so many people change jobs so many times during their careers, pausing to reflect on a work anniversary or even a birthday means a great deal and helps make the work environment worth coming to every day for everyone there. There is nothing wrong—and quite a lot right—with a workplace that has traditions of genuine celebration, and that looks forward to gatherings for birthday cake, bridal and baby showers, and holiday potluck luncheons. It turns out, as well, that when times are tough, as they inevitably are, those are the same workplaces that pull together to recognize a grieving teammate and to help a friend in need. As with every other such piece of advice we have, don't do these things because they work; do these things because they are right and decent. What you will find is that the right and decent way is also the polite way.

Chapter Six

Clients and Client Development: Exceeding Expectations

As law is at its heart a service business, you might think that there is really only one rule—of etiquette, or of anything else—in dealing with existing clients, and acquiring new ones: serve, serve, serve. Indeed, that's a terrific place to start thinking about how to interact with actual and potential clients, but it's only a starting point.

Whenever clients are asked why they like a particular lawyer or law firm, or why they have switched counsel, the answers consistently touch on matters of service, but as seen through the lens of behavior.

Clients assume technical competence; what they want is to have their calls and emails answered promptly, to have their deadlines met (or, if not met, then warned of the impending failure, with plans made for how and when their expectations will be satisfied), and to be dealt with as though their needs—and not their lawyer's—are paramount. In other words, they wish to be treated with respect. Let's discuss some simple rules in the etiquette of dealing with clients—and then tackle some business development situations involving potential clients, as well—to see how respect can be translated into client satisfaction.

Be Available

We are old enough to remember when machines were referred to as "labor-saving devices." By now, the fundamental truth—that our electronic "assistants" are really labor-expanding devices—should be apparent to all. When we started working as lawyers, yes, you were expected to be in the office quite a bit, but when you weren't, you were awfully hard to reach, in a world without the Internet, or email, or cell phones, or even personal fax machines. When you left the office, unless you were at home, it would take a search party with tracker dogs to find you.

Today's world is a very different place, and not necessarily for the better. The ubiquity of electronic accessibility does mean that you can check a baseball score from anywhere on the planet at any time (which is a good thing, for the most part), but it also means that, as Martha and the Vandellas famously sang, there's "nowhere to run to, baby, nowhere to hide." Work can and will find you anywhere at any time. In terms of clients and client development, that means that clients, too, expect their lawyers generally to be available and accessible at all times.

"At all times" is a little bit much, we agree; it may be true that, as Parkinson's Law commands, work expands to fill the time allotted for its completion, but do we really need to allot twenty-four hours a day, seven days a week, to work? No, not really, and we've written elsewhere herein about ways to set aside blocks of time—within the workday and outside it—for other things, work and non-work alike. Still, as we also wrote elsewhere, the price we must pay for being unavailable sometimes (say, while sleeping) is being diligent about being available other times. Check your email and your voicemail periodically; use tools that notify you by email that you have a voicemail; set out-of-office messages that create reasonable expectations for responsiveness even when you are unavailable. Clients appreciate availability as an actual and symbolic commitment to serving their needs more than almost anything else you can do.

Answer the Phone, Please

Even in today's email-addicted world, an unbelievable number of client interactions start with a phone call, one that basically says, "I need help. Can you please help me?" If at all possible, lawyers should answer their own phone. Clients are often incredibly impressed that a lawyer answers his or her own line. It conveys eagerness to help and also a willingness, rather than a reluctance, to take whatever calls come.

Sometimes, of course, it's not possible to answer your own phone, because you're in a meeting, or working on an important drafting assignment or preparation session that requires quiet contemplation. During such times, it's perfectly acceptable to have your assistant answer your phone and for you to be unavailable. Rather than simply leaving your assistant to fend for himself in the face of an insistent client, however, get into the habit of agreeing upon a time at which he'll say you're expected to be free, and then try your best to stick to that time. Clients really appreciate having lawyers who are respectful enough of their clients' time to keep the appointments they make, even when the appointment in question is simply a time at which to return a call.

Sound Excited

Is this really a rule of etiquette? Perhaps not; maybe it's more of a suggestion as to deportment. Whatever it is, though, we can tell you from personal experience that excitement and eagerness—if genuine—come through on the telephone, and so do their opposites, including dread and disdain. Clients really pick up on an excited lawyer (anyone reading this from outside the profession, let us assure you that there are lots of excited, happy lawyers; they're the ones who are comfortable in their own skins), and sensing your excitement makes them want to call you. And creating clients who want to call you is called "client development." This little rule is worth writing down on a sticky note and affixing to the phone; it's that important.

Return Calls Promptly

Now we're clearly back in the realm of etiquette. As a service matter, sooner is better for returning calls; surely within a business day, if at all possible within a very few hours—there's no such thing as "too soon" to return a call from anyone, but most especially a client. Remember that a call from a client is a call for your help, and the entire profession is all about help; even when feeling overwhelmed, you should be grateful for the call and eager (see above) to return it.

An extreme example of this occurred in David's life recently, when he met Donna for an unscheduled midweek dinner out. About halfway through the meal, David's smart-phone began buzzing madly. Did he want to ignore it? Yes. Was dinner with Donna both important and delightful? You bet. But time and experience have taught that a whole bunch of buzzing at 7:30 on a weeknight means that something is up. When David (politely) excused himself after a few moments of this to check, he found (1) a voicemail from a client's CEO, who was in Australia and needed immedi-ate help on a sensitive contract issue, (2) an email from the same CEO, (3) an email from one of the client's directors, saying that the CEO had called him to enlist help in look-ing for David, (4) a voicemail from the same director, to the same effect, and (5) an email from one of David's partners, who represented the director in other matters, saying that the director had called to enlist his help, too, in looking for David. The fact that all of these electronic communica-tions arrived within the space of a single five-minute span is both disturbing and indicative of their importance to the CEO . . . and thus to David, as well. Further excusing him-self, he stood on the street corner outside the restaurant, called the CEO in Australia, and took care of the problem, recognizing both the inconvenience and the importance of promptness; had five more minutes elapsed, that might not have been David's client any longer, but from here on out that's a client who's unlikely to call anyone else.

Respond in Kind

Here's a rule of etiquette for the avoidant personality: Don't return a call with an email, unless expressly requested by the caller to do so. A call conveys so much more than an email, providing tone, pace, the ability to interact in real time, and a chance for you to affect the mental and emotional state of the caller.

Email is severely limited in its ability to do more than convey information; tone is often lost at best, or misconstrued at worst (and yes, all of you wonderful writers who have excelled at every level of education by virtue of your superior wordsmithing abilities, this applies to you, as well; F. Scott Fitzgerald would suffer from the same infirmity, were he writing today and electronically). There will no doubt be times when you return to your desk to find a voicemail from a client that says, "Email me with your availability for a meeting later this week," or something similar, but unless specifically asked to respond in writing, return a call with a call.

Hauling the Mail

When, nonetheless, you are communicating by email, several rules of email etiquette can make your client communications more effective, and thus more welcome and productive.

First and foremost, respond to emails promptly; the medium fairly compels this (indeed, sometimes we respond almost too promptly, with an unguarded reply that we wish we could recall), but lest you be confused on this point, those clients who choose to reach you in writing with the instantaneousness of email expect a prompt response; their choice of medium signals their desire for service. As with returning phone calls, certainly no longer than a single day should elapse between receipt and reply; sooner (much sooner) is better.

Second, respond with brevity if you can. Bearing in mind that email often lacks tone (other than a harsh one), a brief message is more suited to the best use of the medium, conveying factual information (dates, times, names, and jersey numbers). In addition, with email now having gone mobile through the ubiquitous iPhone and similar handheld devices, long messages are often too difficult for clients to read; the handheld screens are small, the circumstances under which the messages are read (furtively in a meeting, or on the train to work, or at a sinfully indulgent—and completely necessary—mid-afternoon baseball game) are not conducive to careful scrolling and word-for-word reading, and thus the chance of misinterpretation increases exponentially.

Third, an email is a piece of writing; treat it as such, and seriously. Use proper grammar and punctuation; communicate in full, thoughtful sentences. Many people treat email as a casual medium of communication, but nothing could be further from the truth. Email is just mail—plain, old-fashioned letter-writing—made quicker and easier by technology. Craft your email as though you mean it.

Finally, email is forever; no matter how sure you are that both sender and recipient have deleted it, it's out there somewhere, on a server, in an archive, just waiting to be produced in response to a discovery request or congressional subpoena. Unless you have drafted your electronic communications with the care and forethought that you'd put into a formal letter, memorandum of law, or legal opinion, the less said the better.

Just Add Water?

As technology has progressed since our first edition of this book, one phenomenon that we must acknowledge and address is that of texting. Given the format, it is almost impossible to enforce against texting the formal-letter-writing rule of etiquette that we propounded for email, but if the audience is a coworker, or more seriously yet, a client, then we would nonetheless urge at least the effort. David has a client who insists upon sending text messages to his cell phone; it takes discipline and judgment for him to follow this rule, but follow it he must. Unless forced as in such circumstances to do so, we would recommend against the use of texting for work-related content.

"Is This Mike On?"

With so many fewer in-person meetings, the conference call has become a staple of the lawyer's life, and often that call takes place by speakerphone. Speakerphones allow you to work hands-free—keeping drafts of several transaction documents before you while you negotiate, taking notes while listening to a conversation, and perhaps including other lawyers and clients in the room with you on one side of the call while facing off against counterparties and opposing counsel on the other side. This terrific tool has its own rules of etiquette, however.

First, be sure to announce multiple parties on your end. A "roll call" at the beginning of a conference call is a very nice way to figure out who is present on the other end of the phone; you should reciprocate by announcing all of the parties on your own end, if possible. There will no doubt be circumstances when someone is a silent participant, and thus unannounced (the junior associate who is joining you for training purposes but not being billed out to the client for the call, for example), but in general, letting everyone know who's on the line is common courtesy, as well as professionally sound behavior.

Second, pick up the handset and go off speaker when you sense the need to do so. If you are on the speakerphone with multiple people in the room with you and a client begins to make a personal aside to you, pick up and take that portion of the conversation out of a too-public forum.

Finally, beware the "mute" button. By now, we've all likely been in circumstances where someone has believed that they have "muted" their end of the call, only to be still audible to the other participants; at best, such a technical malfunction can produce a no-harm, no-foul window into the other side of the conversation, but at worst it can reveal internal deliberations that were intended to be private, or worse still some snarky personal aside that was not meant to be heard. All of the adherence imaginable to the other rules of etiquette cannot undo the damage that an unintended and unmuted snide remark can do in the midst of a delicate negotiation; take appropriate care, and don't become the fodder for someone else's cautionary tale.

Don't Just Be Prompt, Be Early

We've discussed other elements of promptness elsewhere, but they all bear amplification here, when applied to meetings with clients, where they all reduce to one simple rule: Do not be late, period. Ever.

Clients deserve the utmost respect of their time, especially from those of us who happen to be charging them for our own. Strive to be super-prompt, arriving slightly early (five minutes or so should be sufficient) for every single obligation where a client is present. The discipline of planning to be early will save you when circumstances conspire to try to make you late; arriving early will also give you a moment to compose yourself, use the restroom, pop a breath mint, or just meditate. If you must be late, despite your best efforts (if, for example, you have to use any Los Angeles freeway to get to your destination, no matter what the hour of the day), then be sure you have a way to let your client know that you've been delayed, as soon as possible, so that they can use the time in ways other than contemplating how to engage other counsel.

Client Development Tips

Finally, here are a few etiquette-related tips for those on the great quest for that holiest of grails, the new client. Should you be fortunate enough to have a meeting opportunity with a prospective client, four little rules of etiquette will suffice, even if you forget your own name.

First, be prepared; know something about the people and the organization with whom and with which you're meeting, and why you're there. This may not sound like a rule of etiquette, but of course it is; this is merely being respectful of the time of others, specifically the time that they're allotting to speak with you. If you're prepared, then you can help them to use that time productively.

Second, listen more than you speak, especially at first; let them tell you what they want, and then be responsive to their articulated needs. This is the etiquette of deference; it's also a handy way to figure out what you want to say yourself. Formal presentations and pitches are all well and good, but nothing works quite so well as being polite enough to listen to others first.

Third, whether you say it or not, have an attitude of "please." Remember that you're the seeker, no matter how much you may feel that you're in fact being sought for your expertise and experience; many's the lawyer who has lost a potential client who simply could not abide the lawyer's arrogance. You don't need to arrive on bended knee; you must, though, remember to project an attitude of graciousness and humility, and thinking "please," even if you don't say it, will help you to do so.

Finally, say "thank you," both verbally at the end of your meeting and in writing after you return to your office. You've just been given a great gift, namely the opportunity to demonstrate your worthiness and eagerness to help, which, if correctly perceived, may present you with a tangible monetary reward. The very least you can do is say "thank you" and do so correctly, which means not only aloud but also in a written note. Everyone appreciates being appreciated; who's to say that your own gratitude, appropriately expressed, won't be the final push that brings a new client into your practice?

While innumerable books and articles have been written about networking and the job search, we would be remiss not to discuss networking in the context of client development. On this issue, we know a thing or two. Successful client development does not simply happen and it's not a matter of luck. Networking depends upon planning, follow up, and persistence. Here are some tips to guide you through the process with impeccable manners:

Throughout the business world, and in spite of the growing role of technology in our lives (or perhaps because of it), the personal touch matters more than ever; nowhere is this more true than in networking. While social media offer great opportunities to connect online, there is no substitute for an in-person meeting. Meeting face-to-face enables you to really get to know someone and develop a rapport. It's one thing to connect online; it's quite another to break bread together and share stories. One partner at a very successful small law firm regularly arranges networking lunches in her firm's conference room, with fabulous views of Philadelphia. By ordering in, she saves valuable time going to and from her office, and the in-house visits offer a more personalized opportunity to connect. Visits are typically followed by an office tour and the chance to meet other lawyers and staff, so that you leave with a better understanding of this lawyer's work environment and her colleagues. We think that this is a brilliant idea and one worth duplicating.

Networking doesn't just happen; connecting with colleagues, friends, and future clients requires careful planning, often months in advance. Thus, we recommend that you calendar your networking activities. Naturally, you will be putting scheduled get-togethers on your calendar, so that you do not miss them or book conflicting obligations. Beyond that, though, you can calendar follow-up activities as reminders. When a networking meeting

concludes—whether a meal or an informational interview—and you express your thanks (politely) in writing,
plan your next get-together, either by making an appointment right then, or by leaving a reminder to do so on your
calendar around the appropriate future date. Be sure to set
an "alert" on that future meeting, or simply set a second
reminder, between one day and one week prior to the next
meeting, so that you can remember to send a confirming
email. Otherwise, the best-laid plans often get cast aside
when schedules become frenzied.

Successful networking is not merely a series of meetings
and meals; something of value must be exchanged in order
to establish a relationship of trust. At first, that exchange
is likely to be focused on the simple facts of getting to
know one another—your respective backgrounds, skills,
likes, and dislikes. As the relationship deepens, though,
you should be looking for opportunities to help those in
your network, the same way you would seek to help your
friends. Supply helpful information to your network on a
regular basis. As you get to know people, you will begin to
learn about their interests, hobbies, and passions. Keeping
track of this information can be a great way to maintain
connections between in-person meetings. For instance, if
you read about a new production of *Macbeth* and know
that one of your clients is a Shakespeare buff, then by all

means, send along the news with a friendly note. Did you run into a colleague at the newest exercise studio in town? Then let them know about your favorite teacher there. These sorts of friendly, informative exchanges are not only good for business, they are demonstrations of attentiveness and a hallmark of good manners.

While your primary networking approach should be personal and live, technology can play a meaningful supporting role. In addition to using your calendar as a reminder tool, be sure to keep your contacts' information accurate and up to date in your contact database. If you divide the work of policing your contact information with your assistant, then you have an even better chance of staying accurate and current. Further, consider joining a web-based networking tool, such as LinkedIn. Sites such as LinkedIn can offer a streamlined way to both gather information about changes in your contacts' work profiles, and let contacts and colleagues know what you're up to. When used judiciously (and always in conjunction with actual face-to-face socializing), sites such as LinkedIn can be a great boon. It's easy to get started: Access the site of your choice, create a profile by following the prompts, and then begin adding connections. In addition to individual contacts, you can join and participate in LinkedIn groups. Schedule time each week (at the very least) to check your profile, post a comment, congratulate a colleague, and otherwise build your online presence, and stay tuned for update emails from the site that let you know what your contacts are doing. Receiving an email from LinkedIn that tells you that a contact with whom you had lost touch has just changed jobs can be just the motivation you need to send a congratulatory note or make a good luck phone call, which can lead to a celebratory lunch or after-hours get-together, which might in turn be just the time when your contact seeks your thoughts on some new business development, and after that, who knows?

Finally, take some time to pull your nose back from the grindstone, lift your head a bit, and look at your approach from a detached perspective, in order to see what you're really doing. It's awfully easy to get so caught up in the day-to-day details of scheduling meetings, following up, and scheduling next meetings with your ever-expanding network, that you may lose sight of your strategic objectives. From time to time, consider formulating a business plan for yourself. A business plan does not have to resemble the Allies' plan for the invasion of France on D-Day; rather, a one- to five-page outline will suffice. Use the plan as an opportunity to think about your goals—what sorts of work you want to do, with whom you want to work, where you see yourself one or two or five years hence. Then review your current activities, including with whom you're networking. As we have said elsewhere, networking as a cynical, purely goal-driven exercise is unlikely to work as well as networking as a way to build personal relationships of trust (and even if it did work, it doesn't sound to us like a whole heck of a lot of fun), but at the same time, a periodic reexamination of where your network is trending—who you know and like and trust, and the direction that your contacts can take you—is a valuable exercise. Perhaps you will realize that your orientation has been changing without your even being aware. The discipline of periodically assessing where you are and where you are heading can help you find your bearings in a fast-paced, disorienting world.

Chapter Seven

Opposing Counsel:
Dealing Fairly

The question of how to deal with opposing counsel is a thorny one. On the one hand, these are *opposing* counsel—the people on the other side of the table, across the chasm, working every bit as hard to represent their client as zealously as you are (and well they should, as their ethical obligations compel them to do so). In the heat of battle, who's to say that the rule should be anything other than "all's fair in love and war," so long as we stay within the bounds of applicable rules of legal ethics? Indeed, I'm sure that we can all point to many an example of a no-holds-barred, take-no-prisoners practitioner with whom we've gone toe-to-toe, eyeball-to-eyeball, *mano-a-mano*.

On the other hand, does the ethical duty of zealous representation actually compel us to confront opposing counsel as though we were Schwarzenegger in the last reel of any of his films (well, except for *Twins*, and perhaps

Kindergarten Cop)? Whatever happened to the courtly manners of the bar? Is there no place left in our profession for the time-honored custom of professional courtesy?

This being, after all, a book about etiquette for lawyers, it will surprise you not at all that we do, in fact, think that there are—or at least ought to be—rules that can guide us in our interactions with opposing counsel.

"You Catch More Flies with Honey . . . "

Now, we're lawyers, and we do recognize that sharp elbows are sometimes required in order to get through a tough negotiation or a challenging litigation; so be it. But we nonetheless subscribe to the notion that, in general, you can indeed "disagree without being disagreeable."

To the extent possible, try to keep a calm voice in interchanges with opposing counsel; avoid hyperbole and histrionics; and don't shout, scream, literally pound the table with your fist or shoe, or writhe on the floor.

At some point, such behaviors cross the line from merely aggressive to actually theatrical, and thereby lose their effect. While you're screaming bloody murder on a conference call, trust us, the other side has pushed the "mute" button and is probably laughing at how out of control you are. We won't go so far as to say that such tactics never work, but we will say that they work far less frequently and effectively than you might think.

"What Goes Around, Comes Around"

In law, as in poker, there are times when you hold all the right cards (or, as they say in Texas Hold 'Em, "you have the positive nuts"); with leverage comes success, or at least the likelihood of success. But, in law as in poker, after each hand the cards are shuffled and dealt again, and leverage has a funny way of slipping away from you and crossing the table now and again.

So, conduct yourself with opposing counsel in such a manner that, if a tectonic shift happens to occur, you haven't built a reservoir of resentment and lust for revenge that they'll be motivated to crush, kill, and destroy you and your client's position.

David tells his junior colleagues of a representation he once saw, in which a client was investing in a highly touted Internet start-up that was represented by counsel who, shall we say, possessed arrogance in direct proportion to the soaring valuations of his client. He screamed and cried and carried on in the negotiation over the initial investment, and since he had the leverage (everyone wanted to buy into this company), he got a terrific deal for his client.

But things have a way of turning around. A couple of years later the Internet start-up needed more capital from its existing investors, and by then the worm had turned, the market had gone south, the leverage shoe was on the other foot, and the investor who was being asked to pony up new money well remembered the abusive behavior of company counsel. Funnier still, the fellow tried it again, yelling and carrying on during conference calls, trying to scare his client and everyone else half to death. The investor sat stoically through it all, denying point after point that company counsel raised (even the reasonable ones). Don't let this happen to you.

Communications with Parties Known to Be Represented

We all learned in our Legal Ethics course that, if you're communicating with another party whom you know to be represented by counsel, then that opposing counsel must be present for the communication, unless the opposing counsel—not the opposing party—waives the right to participate. Yet, in instance after instance, this rule is forgotten, especially in non-litigation contexts; lawyers seem to call the other side's client directly to ask a due diligence question, or email them directly without copying their lawyers to seek a document or send a new draft, and don't seem to recognize the issue they've created.

The ethical rule against communicating directly with an opposing party known to be represented no doubt stems from an appreciation of the special ability that lawyers have, due to their superior knowledge of the law and of how it can be turned to the advantage of one side or the other, to manipulate or trap the other side when the other side's lawyer isn't present to defend him or her. (One with a more cynical cast of mind might also view this rule as a sort of "lawyers' full employment act," but that strikes us as less than charitable.)

So, it's easy for us to reiterate the ethical rule as a rule of etiquette, as well: Don't communicate with the other side of a case or deal, whom you know to be represented, without going through his or her lawyer.

This means that, when your client calls you and says, "Call so-and-so on the other side, and ask such-and-such," the only right answer is to reply, "Great, I'll call so-and-so's lawyer and ask if we can put together an all-hands conference call." Similarly, when it's time to send a draft contract out to all parties, the other side's lawyer must be copied if his or her client is a recipient; if you don't have the lawyer's contact information, you may call or email the opposing party directly to ask for contact details, but nothing else. Follow the ethical rule, and you'll also be a model of good etiquette.

What happens, though, when you slip up, and despite your best efforts inadvertently send something without copying opposing counsel? Admit your mistake immediately; call the lawyer on the other side and apologize, and then send a personal, handwritten note to reiterate your regret. This doesn't have to be an over-the-top, rend-your-own-garment note; a simple, "I apologize once more for my omission" will serve very nicely. Doing so is not a sign of weakness; the weakness of your error speaks for itself, and to err is human, after all. Rather, it's a sign of self-confidence and a way of re-leveling the playing field; you're taking the other side down from the moral high ground on which you've placed them through your own actions, and thus benefiting your client.

Chapter Eight

Outside Advisors: Working Well Together

Lawyers are frequently called upon to work with third parties in order to accomplish an assignment for a client. Over the course of a day, you may wind up helping a forensic accountant gather materials to analyze a complicated commercial litigation; chatting with tax advisors on a conference call to help structure a complicated international acquisition; speaking with a caregiver who is helping an aged client with a healthcare challenge; collaborating with an environmental consultant while dealing with a real property matter; or just arranging to have the local copy shop duplicate six banker's boxes of deposition exhibits. These are ordinary course commercial transactions and business relationships among service providers; yet, even here, there are rules of conduct and of business etiquette that can help you to achieve better results for yourself and your clients. What are they?

We're All in the Same Boat

At first blush, it may seem to you that outside advisors are just vendors, and are there to do no more than serve you at your pleasure. The temptation to transfer the stress and strain of your own work onto their backs may be enormous; after all, you're getting last-minute calls from clients who are posing impossible challenges and making unreasonable demands, so why shouldn't you do the same yourself when the shoe is on the other foot, and you're effectively the client? Sad but true, everyone is tempted to kick the dog from time to time.

Here's why you should not give in to the temptation to be anything less than gracious in your dealings with outside advisors: Both you and the outside advisor are striving to reach the same goal of serving your mutual client. The etiquette of the situation, therefore, suggests that you treat the advisor as a part of your own team, and not as someone across the table, much less under your heel. Doing so gives you a key to unlock the door to better client service for the client you both share.

An outside advisor who is treated with courtesy and respect—even before that respect has been earned through independent action—is more likely to rise to the occasion and perform up to the level that you require, and that, in turn, will make your life far more easy and worry-free than any flogging before the mast, no matter how cathartic. Outside advisors are no different than your own internal team members; they respond to the same signs of respect, awards of credit, and expressions of gratitude. In the words of the movie of the same title, "pay it forward" and extend to your outside advisors and vendors the same courtesy that you'd wish to receive yourself.

For example, in the world of transactional work, there are many different outside advisors who may contribute to a deal: Accountants may conduct financial and accounting due diligence; benefits advisors may contribute analysis of employee benefit plans; insurance consultants may analyze the adequacy of coverage and coordinate policy transfers; and environmental engineers may conduct investigations and testing for the presence of hazardous materials. During the course of a deal, you may have to work with all of these parties to bring the transaction to a successful conclusion; treating each as though they were part of your own internal team will help keep everyone focused and in synch. When it's the night before closing and you need that insurance consultant to stay late and work a little magic to make sure that the target's policies are assigned properly and that the new lender is named as an additional insured, they'll be a whole lot more likely to take your call and help you out if they've been treated as peers and not as peons.

Listen and Learn

Beyond mere responsiveness and performance, outside advisors and vendors have a perspective of their own to add, and can educate you in how to meet client expectations more fully; thus, the second rule of etiquette is to open your ears and listen politely to what third-party vendors have to say. After all, they see a variety of different lawyers and other service providers in their own work; they know what succeeds and what fails. You can learn much from those who are interacting with your clients on a different level; polite inquiry with an attitude of deference and respect will someday yield a pearl or two of wisdom that will improve your own client service and repay your kindness many times over.

Fostering a team approach with outside advisors should extend beyond the specific case or deal on which you are working; the benefits of expanding and deepening the relationship are enormous. For example, consider scheduling a separate, in-person "after-action" meeting between your team and each advisor; this provides an opportunity for you both to uncover mutual "lessons learned" and also to build one-on-one connections between team members on both sides at all levels. As everyone is working to expand their personal networks and find compatible relationships on which to build their careers, meetings such as this can provide many meaningful opportunities to build under-standing and trust, and to prepare the ground for the next encounter; you already have the relationship, and a common history and topics of conversation, so all of the awkward and difficult initial contact is behind you.

Also consider putting together teach-ins for each other's broader teams on topics of interest; many outside advisors are eager to come in to give a lunch-and-learn presenta-tion, often with continuing legal education credit, as a way of broadening their own networks. Joint presentations to common clients can also help to cement relationships both with the client and with each other; clients, too, are eager to hear something genuinely new and valuable, and will often make time for their already-trusted outside legal and other advisors to come in and speak, at the same time that competing service providers are knocking on their doors in vain. Partnering to build and keep a mutual client rela-tionship can be valuable for everyone.

Start Spreading the News

Finally, outside advisors can be their own pathways to busi-ness development, and thus are worthy of being treated as worth their weight in gold. You never know when that environmental consultant will be speaking with some prospective client of whom you've never even dreamt, and hearing about that prospect's woes with other counsel. When that happens, you want to be in a position for that advisor to recount what a terrific relationship they've seen you have with your clients and those clients' whole teams, including service providers.

Despite the advances of technology and the retreats of advertising, law is still very much a business based on personal contacts; to rise to the level of being a client's trusted advisor, you often need to start by being recommended by another. Word of mouth is the most important client development tool you have. Make sure that the positive buzz about you is heard from all directions, including outside service providers, by treating them all in so respectful a manner that speaking well of you becomes second nature to them.

Chapter Nine

Office Events: Socializing
with Civility

Socializing as part of your work life enables you to enjoy time with colleagues, staff members, and clients in a more relaxed environment. After-hours events blend work and leisure: On the one hand, you are spending time with work colleagues; on the other hand, you are outside the office, at a sports event, birthday party, or other celebration. As a result, determining what's appropriate and what's inappropriate can be a little challenging.

The golden rules of etiquette (see chapter twelve) apply at all times. Good manners do not take a holiday simply because you are socializing outside the office, whether with colleagues, clients, or potential clients.

Respond in a Timely Manner

When you receive an invitation, check the date on your calendar and determine if you can attend. One of the easiest ways to show courtesy to others is to respond to an invitation in a timely manner. An invitation that requests an R.S.V.P. means please respond "yes" or "no" by a certain date. An invitation that says "regrets only" means just that: Only respond if you cannot attend; otherwise we will assume that you will be present.

Making office staff chase you down for an answer is poor behavior and smacks of self-importance. No matter how busy you may be, respond and keep your commitment. If your work or travel schedule prohibits a prompt response, delegate the responsibility to your professional assistant.

Determine Who Is Invited to the Event

If an invitation is addressed to you only, then you are the only invitee. If you and your spouse or partner or "and guest" are listed on the address line, then you are both invited. If your name and the words "and family" appear on the address line, then by all means bring the whole gang to the festivities. In any event (no pun intended), do not bring an uninvited guest to an event. If you have any questions, simply ask the individual organizing the event for guidance.

Understand Who Will Be at the Event

It helps to prepare for an office event if you know who may be there. Is this event for lawyers only? Lawyers and staff? Everyone's families? Will firm clients be present? If so, will any of your clients be present? These are worthwhile questions to ask in order to be prepared to socialize and make everyone comfortable.

Appropriate Attire

Should you have any question about the appropriate attire for an event, call beforehand and ask. In most cases, office events take place directly after work, and this presupposes that business attire or business casual, depending on your office, is both expected and acceptable. However, if you are struggling with the precise definition of "casual chic" or "festive attire," then ask before the event so as to avoid embarrassment to yourself and your host.

Never wear anything too revealing or risqué. Anything too tight, too revealing, or too short may be great for personal time, but you do not want to be remembered by your colleagues or clients for being the person who wore the unusual outfit. This goes for gentlemen, as well as ladies; we have seen that free-spirited fellow who has shown up at a summer jacket-and-tie event wearing Bermuda shorts and sockless penny loafers with his blazer and club tie, and yes, that is über-preppy, but play it safe and stick with khakis, please (no matter how great you think your getup would look at Old Nassau). Your goal is to be remembered for your great attitude, not your bizarre attire.

Fashionably Late versus Inexcusably Late

For large parties or other group gatherings with a cocktail hour preceding the event, fashionably late means that you can arrive up to fifteen minutes after the stated start time. After fifteen minutes you enter the domain of inexcusably late.

For sit-down dinners, ascertain the start time from the host or hostess in order to determine what fashionably late means. For some individuals, a stated time to begin dinner is the time the event begins. Period. You don't want to walk into a room with everyone seated and enjoying their appetizers. Ask beforehand to avoid embarrassment.

For theater performances, lectures, and the like, arrive ten minutes early and leave ample time to find your seat, chat a few moments, and then enjoy the show. You do not want to be one of the latecomers seated at the discretion of the manager, particularly when you are attending an event as a representative of your firm.

Tips for Socializing with Style

While entire books have been written about how to navigate social events, the following are some useful tips to keep in mind. Donna recommends Susan RoAne's *The Secrets of Savvy Networking*, a smart, in-depth advice book for those seeking detailed information, as well as the resources created by Diane Darling and her team at Effective Networking, Inc. (www.EffectiveNetworking.com).

- **Be the host (even if you're not the host).** One of the best ways to take control of a social situation is to pretend that you are hosting the event and in charge of making people feel comfortable. This is a great trick and it really works. Rather than stand idly by, make yourself the official greeter and seater. Make it a point to say hello, introduce yourself, and—if the event is one with open seating—invite someone to sit with you. When you stop focusing on yourself and start focusing on others, you will be amazed at the quality of interactions that follow.

- **Make introductions.** People assume that everyone knows everyone else. This is a huge assumption to make, particularly at very large law firm events. Act as the informal emcee and make sure you introduce people. Never assume that Person A knows Person B. Here's how to do it: "John, I want you to meet Fred, the new tax associate who just started with us. John is a senior associate in the litigation department. Fred, meet John."

- **Recover from name amnesia.** You can't remember a person's name. You're embarrassed. They look so familiar, but you don't know how you know them. You're too young to have Alzheimer's and your head injury healed years ago. What do you do? Don't panic. Everyone forgets names. We've been known to forget our own child's name from time to time (tip: "hey, you" works fine). Simply turn to the person in question, smile, and say, "I am so sorry, but please tell me your name again." Then—here's the key—stop, look at the person and really listen to the name they tell you. Then repeat the person's name and say, "Fran, that's right . . . nice to see you again." (Obviously, that particular one only works if the person's name is, in fact, Fran.) If you're really good, you'll repeat the name in your head a few times and try to create a connection, like Fran with the deep tropical tan, or something like that.

- **Pay attention.** When conversing with one or more people, make those people the focus of your attention. No looking at your watch. No roving eye to see if someone better walks into your line of vision. People notice when others' attention is drifting, and it's impolite. Instead, make it a point to pay full attention to the person in front of you before scanning the room for friends.

- **Avoid breaking into conversations.** It can be very daunting to walk into a room of strangers and expect to engage people in conversation. This can be particularly hard when people are gathered in small groups and seem to be having a jolly time without you. In our experience, it's wise to avoid approaching pairs engaged in conversation. Typically, two people standing close with their heads together are having a personal conversation. Unless one of the individuals catches your eye and beckons you to join them, look for groups of three or more. Stand at the periphery and try to make eye contact. This is where the edict to "be the host" can be so important. Look for someone to catch your eye, smile, and beckon you to join them.

- **Avoid eating and drinking distractions.** While we discussed sit-down meals in chapter one, it's worth touching upon the issue of how to balance the wine glass and the appetizer plate, while maintaining a free hand to greet people. The simplest solution, in our opinion, is to enjoy a snack beforehand so that you're not hitting the buffet to the exclusion of socializing. Hold a beverage in your left hand and keep your right hand free to shake hands. Problem solved.

- **Be cautious with jokes.** Jokes are no laughing matter when they hit upon the forbidden topics of politics, race, religion, or sexual preference. If you have a good sense of humor and can remember a few "clean" jokes, then joke to your heart's content. Casual observations of a humorous nature are always appropriate. However, be cautious when telling off-color jokes. What if you are the recipient of an off-color joke? It's the height of bad manners to put another person in the uncomfortable position of having to react to something tasteless or offensive. This can be further complicated when the joke-teller is someone in a position of power over you. Do you risk offending the managing partner by saying, "I find that offensive"? Use good judgment in these cases. When a peer tells an off-color joke, express your displeasure politely:

"That's not appropriate and it's not funny, Jane." If the joke-teller is a senior person, acknowledge it quietly and move on.

- **Exchange business cards.** A lawyer should always carry business cards, because networking opportunities can happen anywhere. There is, however, an art to furnishing a business card and some do's and don'ts. For example, furnish a business card after you have spoken with an individual for at least a few minutes and established a connection. Putting business cards on tables or leaving them for the waitstaff to find later is not effective. Donna once attended a large networking luncheon where a real estate agent literally walked from table to table tossing her business cards in the center of each table. No attempt was made to engage the table in discussion or to make a personal introduction; she simply dumped her cards and walked away. Not only was it weird behavior, she had those awful business cards with one's photo on them. There's a better, more meaningful way to exchange business cards. First, engage the person in a conversation, then finish your conversation and say, "I'd love to follow up with you . . . do you have a business card?" That's the opportunity to hand your business card to the person. Take a moment and look at the card; don't simply put it away without a glance. Examine the card briefly and, if possible, make a sincere comment ("that's a nice design" or "what a cool job title" or something that shows you are paying attention). Business cards ought not be furnished at funerals, during hospital visits, and anywhere else that feels inappropriate. Not only can furnishing business cards in hospitals or funeral parlors be construed as soliciting clients (and a violation of the Rules of Professional Conduct), but it's just abysmal manners.

- **Exit with grace.** Ideally, at networking events you want to chat for fifteen or twenty minutes and then move along and meet more people. Don't monopolize other peoples' time and don't allow yourself to be monopolized. How can you extricate yourself from a conversation? Here are some tried-and-true exit lines: "I'm going to refresh my drink," "I have to see if this call is the transplant surgeon (hold phone in hand)," or "Excuse me, it's been a pleasure chatting." Smile and move on.

Specific Socializing Scenarios
The Office Holiday Party

It may be "the most wonderful time of the year," but it's also the time of the year when the most egregious behavior happens. This is, in part, due to holiday cheer and an abundance of eggnog. When you attend the office holiday party, keep in mind a few common-sense rules of etiquette:

- Enjoy a drink or two, but don't become drunk. Once you are inebriated, your ability to make good decisions about proper behavior is greatly reduced. You may not remember what you did when you were drunk, but your colleagues will remember forever.

- Consider serving as a designated driver or, if you know you will be consuming alcohol, have a designated driver on hand or arrange transportation home. Not only is it impolite to drive while intoxicated, it's also illegal.

- Dress appropriately (see above). Try, if at all possible, to avoid Santa hats but, by all means, sport the preppy, holiday-themed trousers with the Christmas trees and a tartan bow tie (come on, 'tis the season!).

- Engage in polite conversation and learn the art of small talk. *What Do I Say Next? Talking Your Way to Business and Social Success*, by Susan RoAne, contains excellent advice to help you converse with ease.

The Summer Associate Event

Many mid-sized and large law firms still offer summer associate events and ask attorneys to participate and represent the firm. Whether it is a cocktail party, dinner event, or family picnic, you may be asked to attend, represent the firm, and meet summer associates.

Your role, as an attorney, is to represent the firm in the best light possible. This means:

- Engage summer associates in pleasant conversation;
- Ask about their law school experiences; and
- Answer questions as candidly as possible while remembering that you are a representative of the firm.

If you are a summer associate, your role is to enjoy the festivities without embarrassing yourself by speaking in tongues, dressing inappropriately, grooming yourself publicly, chewing tobacco, or soiling yourself.

The Client Social Event

Clients may invite you to a holiday party, a product launch, a social dinner with spouses, or a charity golf outing. Similarly, you may be in a position to invite clients to socialize outside regular office hours. These types of events offer excellent opportunities to solidify relationships in an informal environment. All of the aforementioned tips apply to client social events: Dress appropriately, drink in moderation (or not at all), engage in pleasant conversation, and be sure to thank the host or hostess afterward.

An important aspect of client entertaining is to reciprocate in a timely manner. Hence, if you are invited to a holiday party, then be sure to calendar a date to call after New Year's and initiate a lunch together and so forth. If you are new to client entertaining, seek help from a mentor or more senior attorney. It's poor etiquette to always be the guest and never the host.

When entertaining clients, bear in mind your firm's expense reimbursement policies. Just because you are (or may be) entertaining on the firm's tab, doesn't mean that the sky's the limit. Be sensible with your choice of venue. Specifically, be prudent with your choice of wine; the pricier selections on a wine list can quickly take your bill to stratospheric levels, incurring not only the scrutiny but also the wrath of whoever must approve expenses. The best advice here is to treat client entertainment as though you were paying for it yourself (and, if all else fails, if your firm does not reimburse client entertainment in whole or in part, then consider whether you should actually just pay for it yourself; you're investing in your own career, as much as in the firm's relationship, after all).

The Office Farewell Party

One of your colleagues is leaving the firm and there is a party, whether with a cake in the conference room or dinner at a nearby restaurant. If your schedule permits, take the time to attend—even for a brief amount of time—and wish your colleague well. It is good manners to acknowledge another's transition. Furthermore, keeping in touch with former colleagues may also be a great networking experience for you, either in the event that you, too, seek to make a transition, or in the event that you want to cultivate new business.

Express Your Thanks

After any social event, it is appropriate for you to seek out the individual(s) who planned and produced the event to say, "Thank you, you did a good job." The hours of behind-the-scenes work to produce a firm-wide holiday party, summer associate event, or any celebration are enormous and nerve-wracking. You need not write a formal thank-you note, but a sincere verbal "thank you" and an email the next day can go a long way in making a person feel valued.

One final note: If any detail of the event was not to your satisfaction (the food choices were inadequate, the room was too loud, the sound system deficient), save the criticism for later. Public criticism, as well as written criticism, is never polite and always hurtful. If you have something constructive to say, make time to take the person aside afterward and express yourself civilly in person with the office door closed.

Chapter Ten

After Hours: Out On Your Own

Good manners extend beyond one's office hours. Out on your own, you are still bound by the golden rules of etiquette. As an officer of the court and a representative of the legal profession in your community, you have a responsibility to project a level of professionalism and civility at all times. Your days of cow tipping are over, counselor.

Your behavior will reflect upon you and your employer, as well as the profession generally. Therefore, always exercise sound judgment when it comes to questions of behavior. By and large, this means:

Exercise Discretion at All Times

No one is asking a lawyer to lead a life of monk-like abstinence in duty to the profession. You will entertain clients, family, and friends (not necessarily all together), attend bachelor or bachelorette parties, and otherwise engage in an active, engaging social life. Moderation is the key. Indulge and blow off steam in a socially appropriate way. Damning photos, blog entries, or newspaper articles ought not trumpet your exploits. Nor should your reputation among your peers evince their belief that you are inappropriate or otherwise unseemly in your private life. Discretion in all matters ought to be the watchword for you and your social life.

Drink in Moderation

While enjoying alcohol is typically part and parcel of after-hours socializing, keep in mind that you ought to drink in moderation and never lose control. Not only is drunkenness an unattractive state of being, it leads to patently illegal activities, including driving while under the influence. Consume alcohol in moderation and maintain your reputation among peers and outsiders alike. Another perfectly acceptable alternative is to not drink at all.

Keep Your Word

When you promise to attend an event, contribute to a charity, or offer help, be reliable and worthy of one's trust.

Avoid saying "yes" and then backing out of obligations. Instead, be honest and forthright about your time and resources before making a commitment. People will respect an individual who takes on fewer obligations but follows through thoroughly more than the individual who says "yes" and does not fulfill his or her commitments. Your trustworthiness matters, and your reputation in these matters will extend beyond the profession.

Volunteer within Your Community

Offering your services pro bono, serving on a board of directors for a community initiative, or volunteering your time for a cause that impassions you are all wonderful ways of giving back and showing respect for those in your community. Take the time, even early in your legal career, to find a volunteer opportunity that interests you and get involved.

Chapter Eleven

Moving On: The Etiquette of Changing Jobs

Throughout one's career there will be many opportunities to change firms, agencies, corporations, and even professions. Retention and attrition studies bear out the fact that lawyers change jobs with considerable frequency. A study by the NALP Foundation entitled, "Keeping the Keepers II: Mobility and Management of Associates," reported that within the first two years of practice, nearly a quarter of the associates at law firms of all sizes have moved on. After five years, more than half of those hired out of law school have left their original firms.

With the knowledge that the legal profession is increasingly mobile, be open to the possibility of change. Networking serves many purposes, both in terms of personal fulfillment and professional practicality. Maintaining ties with college and law school classmates, law firm alums, and friends will help you explore other career options when the time is ripe.

Since so many positions are filled through word of mouth, it makes sense to foster those connections on a regular basis. With that in mind, be sure to tend your network of contacts with social lunches and friendly telephone calls and emails, as well as holiday correspondence. While you ought not be nice for the sake of an ulterior motive, you should keep your contacts apprised of your career path generally.

In particular, treat legal search professionals (headhunters) with respect when they contact you. Take headhunters' calls and speak briefly and politely no matter how busy you may be. You may not be interested in a different job opportunity today, but your career plans may change. If you are pleased with your employment situation today, simply say, "Thanks for calling, but I'm happy with my situation right now." Burning bridges by being rude, sarcastic, or nasty will not benefit you in the long run since you cannot know what the future holds.

Job change and etiquette are not mutually exclusive concepts. It is possible—and preferable—to transition from one employer to another while maintaining one's good manners. The following are some suggestions for leaving an employer on good terms:

Never Denigrate a Former Employer

Even if you left under less-than-optimal circumstances, never denigrate a former employer. Short-circuit any negative commentary by saying, "it wasn't a good fit" or "I was looking for a different type of practice environment."

Never Denigrate a Former Employee

Avoid speaking negatively about former colleagues or staff professionals. First, you never know who another person knows or is related to, and unkind words will, no doubt, travel far. Second, nothing is gained by tarnishing another person's good name. Finally, bad-mouthing a former employee could result in legal action. In short, do not speak ill of the departed.

Give Appropriate Notice Before Your Departure (But Be Prepared to Depart the Day You Announce Your New Position)

Give your employer at least four weeks' notice; however, you ought to be prepared to exit your office the day of your announcement. While some firm policies will vary (and certainly circumstances of departures will vary greatly and cannot be generalized here), you should assume that you may be asked to depart the premises the day of your announcement. Therefore, prepare carefully so your exit— should it happen more suddenly than you imagined—is as dignified as possible.

Adhere to the Rules of Professional Conduct Regarding Client Files

Whether you leave to join another firm or to start your own practice, adhere to the Rules of Professional Conduct pertaining to client files and client confidentiality. You may not copy client files or other information. You may not contact clients for the purpose of soliciting them to change firms prior to actually leaving your current employer.

Failure to adhere to the rules in your jurisdiction is not only a breach of the Rules of Professional Conduct, but a poor reflection on you as an individual. Prior to switching employers, review the Rules and be sure to adhere to them carefully so as to avoid any conflicts.

Chapter Twelve

Conclusion: The Golden Rules of Etiquette

We've considered etiquette for the legal practitioner in a wide range of settings, and we've seen many and varied examples of how proper etiquette can make a lawyer's life smoother and more pleasant, as well as examples of how the absence of etiquette can lead to disagreeable, even disadvantageous, outcomes.

We hope that, at this point in our tale, the reasons to integrate politeness and good manners into your everyday work life are clear and compelling, and that the manner in which to do so has been amply demonstrated. Still, we would like to leave you with a set of guidelines, which combine both theory and practice, to help you know what to do in almost any situation, or to know why you should act in a particular way so that you can deduce the appropriate behavior yourself. We call these the "Golden Rules of Etiquette."

Etiquette Is Empathy

The first and most important Golden Rule of Etiquette is the "golden rule" itself: Do unto others as you would have them do unto you. Whether you learned this principle from its Old Testament origins, from its New Testament revival, from another of the many religious and secular sources that incorporate this notion, or just from plain old-fashioned common sense, if you can internalize this fundamental concept, then you're already more than halfway to your destination in any situation that demands a well-mannered response or behavior.

All we're really encouraging is that each of us take the time to place ourselves in the shoes of another (the colleague with whom we're working on a case, the client who's waiting for an answer, the opposing counsel who's across the table from us in a deal, the stranger in the elevator), and then act in such a manner as to make that person comfortable, as we ourselves would want to be comfortable in those circumstances. Most questions of etiquette truly can be resolved by making them into simple questions of empathy, without knowing a single other "rule."

Etiquette Is Also Respect

Our empathic approach presumes that the way we would want to be treated in the shoes of another would be with respect—not for our position, rank, seniority, wealth, status, or caste, but rather for ourselves as a fellow human being. The notion of etiquette would be turned on its head, were we to imagine etiquette as a set of behaviors founded on the notion that the way people want to be treated is with contempt or derision or dismissiveness.

Etiquette as respect does not attach merely to a person, but also to everything about their situation: their time, their responsibilities, the competing demands to which they are subject, their role within an organization or a community or a family.

Etiquette Is a Social Lubricant

Etiquette makes it possible for people who don't have their own independent relationships of trust and respect with one another to nonetheless interact with a minimum of friction, because they each do what's more or less expected in any given circumstance. Such a lubricant can help lead to true respect, and later to actual trust, as the parties build confidence in one another over a longer course of interaction. Without etiquette (even the *ad hoc* variety based on empathy without set rules), our mercurial natures could easily undermine confidence and leave us isolated and ineffective.

Etiquette Disarms

Etiquette makes it more difficult for a counterparty to summon outrage or anger or raised voices in service of their argument. A polite and quiet approach to tense interactions can create either an induced sense of complacency or intense frustration and disorientation on the other side of the interchange; either can create opportunities to turn a situation to the benefit of the more well-behaved party.

Etiquette Conveys Forethought

We all look smarter than we are when that extra instant taken to manage an interaction with a modicum of grace suggests that we know what we're doing and what effect we're having on others and that we're mature and careful enough to handle anything that comes our way. Etiquette can help us not merely rise to the occasion, but rather create occasions that rise to us.

Etiquette Is Not an Altruistic Behavior

In fact, etiquette is just as much about self-interest as it is concerned with anyone else. Because etiquette comforts the recipient of well-mannered behavior, eases the path, and builds confidence, its application necessarily benefits the practitioner.

We very much hope that these *Modern Rules of Business Etiquette* help to guide you in the many and varied circumstances in which you will no doubt find yourself, where well-mannered behavior may be the difference between success and failure. We trust that this resource has done nothing more than to reinforce your own best tendencies and good sense; from time to time, we all need to see the right thing to do written out for us, simply to confirm that we've not been made crazy by the insane pace and pressure of our modern world. Rather than codifying a crusty old set of rules, we would like to believe that these more organic principles can reflect the best elements of professionalism and common sense that have been part of the practice of law since the start, embodying respect for clients, colleagues, fellow practitioners, and society. We look forward to crossing paths with all of you . . . politely.

For Further Reading

Fine, Debra. *The Fine Art of Small Talk*. Hyperion, 2005.

Forni, P.M. *Choosing Civility: The Twenty-Five Rules of Considerate Conduct*. New York: St. Martin's Press, 2002.

Professor P.M. Forni of Johns Hopkins University offers a true gem for readers. Forni's twenty-five rules for connecting effectively with others is a model for well-mannered behavior in all situations.

Fox, Sue. *Etiquette for Dummies*. New York: Wiley Publishing, 1999.

Part of the popular *For Dummies* series, Sue Fox's book uses humor to cover the gamut of etiquette situations, including how to communicate graciously at home and at work, and proper behavior at weddings and formal events.

Gerson, Donna. *Building Career Connections: Networking Tools for Law Students and New Lawyers*. NALP, 2007.

Kaplan, Ari. *The Opportunity Maker*. West, 2008.

Post, Peggy, and Peter Post. *The Etiquette Advantage in Business (2nd edition)*. New York: HarperCollins Publishers, 2005.

This book provides excellent general information for business etiquette in the workplace, in social settings, with clients, and throughout the interview process.

Post, Peggy. *Everyday Etiquette: Practical Advice for Social Situations at Home and on the Job*. New York: HarperPaperbacks, 1999.

Peggy Post offers practical advice for a range of situations, from silverware to thank-you notes, replying to invitations, making condolence calls, and other day-to-day issues.

Post, Peggy. *"Excuse Me, But I Was Next . . .": How to Handle the Top 100 Manners Dilemmas*. New York: HarperCollins Publishers, 2006.

Peggy Post catalogues the top 100 etiquette questions with simple, concise answers.

RoAne, Susan. *What Do I Say Next? Talking Your Way to Business and Social Success*. New York: Warner Books, 1997.

This informative, funny guide teaches you the secrets of talking your way to business and social success. RoAne addresses how to navigate social settings with ease.

RoAne, Susan. *How to Work a Room*. New York: Warner Books, 1989.
A wonderful, witty discussion of how to socialize and put yourself, and others, at ease.

Shipley, David, and Will Schwalbe. *Send: The Essential Guide to Email for Office and Home*. New York: Alfred A. Knopf, 2007.
This primer on communications offers important information on email etiquette for business.

Online Resources

Diane Darling (Effective Networking, Inc.) provides helpful resources through her website, www. EffectiveNetworking.com. Become more comfortable in social situations, and you will sharpen your etiquette skills.

Andrea Nierenberg's website and blog, www.
nierenberggroup.com, offers great advice about social
skills, networking, and business development.

Index